The Plastics Handbook

A RotoVision Book

Published and distributed by RotoVision SA
Route Suisse 9
CH-1295 Mies
Switzerland

RotoVision SA
Sales and Editorial Office
Sheridan House, 114 Western Road
Hove BN3 1DD, UK

Tel: +44 (0)1273 72 72 68
Fax: +44 (0)1273 72 72 69
www.rotovision.com

10 9 8 7 6 5 4 3 2 1

ISBN: 978-2-88893-002-0

Art Director Tony Seddon
Design by Ginny Zeal

Reprographics in Singapore by
ProVision Pte.
Tel: +65 6334 7720
Fax: +65 6334 7721

Printed in China by Midas Printing
International Ltd.

The Plastics Handbook

Chris Lefteri

RotoVision

Contents

Contents

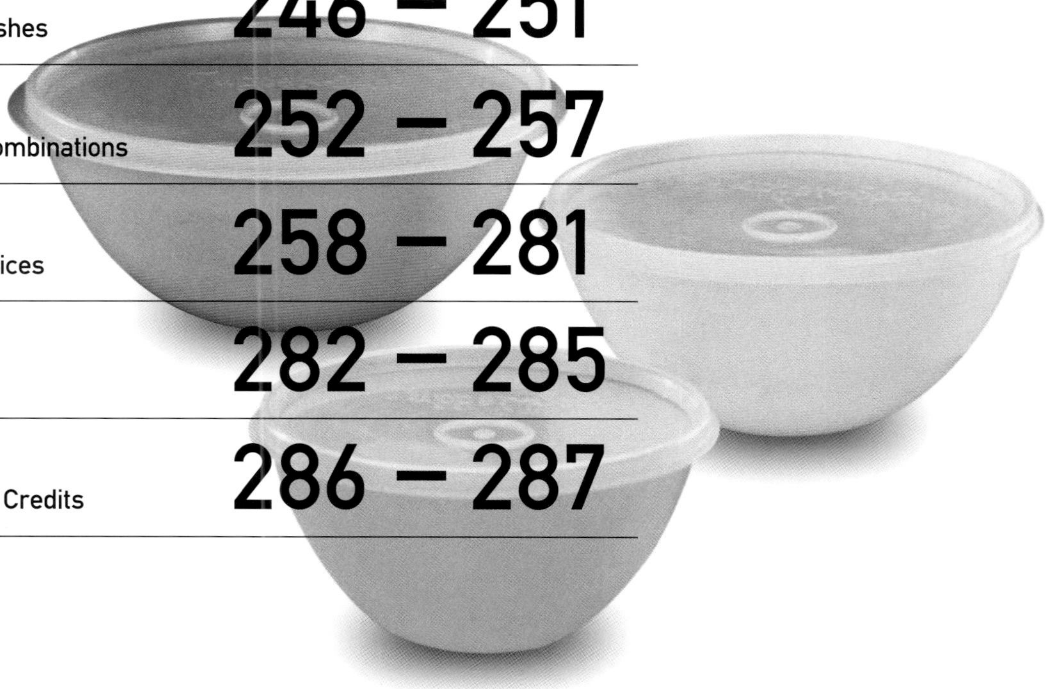

Introduction

The world of plastic continues to grow at a rapid rate—not so much in new formulations, but defiantly in new applications, new technologies, and new composites.

So where is this colossal group of plastic materials moving as it continues to carve its way through every part of our lives? How do we track these new developments, and how do they shift our definition of an industry that continues to evolve so rapidly?

In the broadest terms, plastics form a group of materials that is defined by its ability to be easily shaped, but with new composite materials appearing, merging plastics with metals and woods, and infiltrating industries such as glass and ceramics, plastic is not only easily shaped but also a melting pot of crossovers. This is a challenge to how we define plastics in terms of their use, applications, and cultural significance. What role will plastics have in enhancing values and emotions in our future products, and also in fulfilling the ecological considerations that are becoming ever more important? After all, the world of materials is a diverse place: sometimes it is all about technical details; on other occasions the issues are primarily cultural. Sometimes the debates revolve around global trends and shifts, while in the case of wood and ceramics, they are more usually about local concerns.

For designers, plastic is an infinitely adaptable material, which easily takes on complex shapes—a material with the latent potential to be squeezed, pulled, injected, foamed, and sandwiched. In his seminal book *The Material of Invention*, Ezio Manzini talks of materials in transformation. He compares trying to capture a snapshot of materials to taking a group photograph where everyone is in a constant state of movement. This great analogy expresses the difficulty of trying to capture not just the essence of a group of materials that contains thousands of variables, but also how to record them. From a different perspective Roland Barthes describes

plastic thus, "more than a substance, plastic is the very idea of its infinite transformation; as its everyday name indicates, it is ubiquity made visible."

This book examines some of the most important research in the field of plastics, and how these are explored in relation to a broad range of products. Within this book there are iconic plastic products, and also materials such as Velcro, a semiformed plastic that lacks the neatness of classification as molding, fixing mechanism, tape, or textile. Plastic epitomizes mass production and low cost, while also being a material of "infinite transformation."

But some of the strongest additions to the family of plastic materials are from the area of ecological plastics. Plastics that are not only derived from rapidly renewable sources, but are also biodegradable and compostable. Here the definition of plastics is shifting from being the environmental criminal to a material that comes from nature and returns to nature. With these new

materials manufacturers are, for the first time, having to think about how to unmake the products that they have become so efficient at making. The book illustrates and presents a number of producers internationally who are making biopolymers from agricultural products, such as corn. One of the biggest markets for these new environmental plastics is in the packaging industry, where the issue of ecofriendly disposal is increasingly a major focus and, for some companies, a brand differentiator.

The ecological issue is also being dealt with from a recycling perspective. The millions of PET bottles that get discarded every day are now being shredded and turned into insulation for ski jackets or carpets, for example. This new area of "reclaimers" is about finding new uses for old materials—not just from retired products, but also from the waste material of other industries, like wood-plastic composites that use sawdust from the conversion of softwood timber combined with a polymer resin to make injection-moldable components.

More than any other material, perhaps, plastic is too attached to the products that are derived from it. Unlike metal, glass, wood, or ceramic, the image of plastic is often accompanied by the representation of cheap, shiny products, or disposable packaging. When we think of landfill sites, however, we think of plastic products rather than the material itself. Plastic suffers from being too good at its job, from being used without any sense of what will happen to the material when the product is no longer useful.

The book also contains examples that challenge this image of plastic as the material of mass production. In this arena designers are continuing to look at nontraditional approaches to the production of plastic as a high-volume material. In this case, the definition of plastic as a material shifts from mass produced, identical units to the individual and personal, and with the rise in the use of rapid prototyping it is reasonable to assume that the entirely personalized product will soon be upon us. Already

this can be observed to a degree in the introduction of new processing technologies, such as overmold decoration that is used to add decorative surfaces to products, personalizing them for local, cultural, and social markets. Here the expense of retooling is eliminated and plastic is given both new life and new sensorial possibilities by being allied with emotive materials such as metals, woods, and fabrics.

But plastic is also becoming more of an emotive material in its own right, one that has value as a communication tool and is able to be controlled, branded, and design-protected by the global OEMs (original equipment manufacturers), so that the material is seen as part of the product branding. Of course, the ability to mold or manufacture previously impossible shapes has meant that form-making as an expression of brand is a well-trodden area. What is perhaps more interesting, however, is the possibility for companies to explore their brand through not only the surface qualities of materials, but also the use

of intelligent surfaces, or more emotive tools such as aromatic additives—a technology that exists, but which is largely unexplored territory. This area of emotive communication combined with the emerging use of nanotechnology, perhaps, may provide a platform for plastics to take on completely new meanings, functions, and roles, which essentially means that plastics will flow and weld themselves completely into other material families. These new hybrids may provide a path to an ultimate material where all technologies melt into a single form of plastic, or lead to a time when the opposite is true, when we have so many variations that the current definitions of woods, metals, glass, and plastics vanish from our vocabulary and lose their meaning.

But the purpose of this book is to provoke you into questioning and thinking about a selection of what I think are some of the most interesting, original, and sometimes just plain fun plastics and plastic products in the world today.

011 Surface

Color is not often the main priority in a designer's specification. It tends to fall some way behind form and material on the sketch sheet, and often appears as the dressing once the other details are in order. However, the importance of color in design should never be understated.

Color is one of the first things we notice when we look at an object. It is also one of the main driving forces behind trends, and can provide the revamping of a product's identity without the need to completely retool the product itself.

Through the addition of a masterbatch, designers have a limitless range of possibilities for color and decoration. Masterbatches are additives to any number of molded plastic products that serve to enhance performance and/or add color and detail.

Snap was created as an alternative to the plastic color samples that are traditionally sent out to designers. The object, consisting of 60 identical components that show the 18 colors, was created by Tom Dixon for Gabriel-Chemie, to highlight the potential for color in the molding of plastics.

Exploring color's full potential

Dimensions	**360mm diameter**
Features	**Decoration is embedded into the surface, which eliminates the possibility of colors being worn or scratched off**
	Not limited to color; can be extended to other effects or additional properties
More	**www.tomdixon.net; www.gabriel-chemie.com**
Applications	**Various masterbatches include antimicrobial additives to enhance strength and durability, wear resistance, environmental resistance, plasticizers to soften plastics, and a range of decorative effects.**

Snap Pentakis Dodecahedron
Designer: Tom Dixon
Manufacturer: Gabriel-Chemie

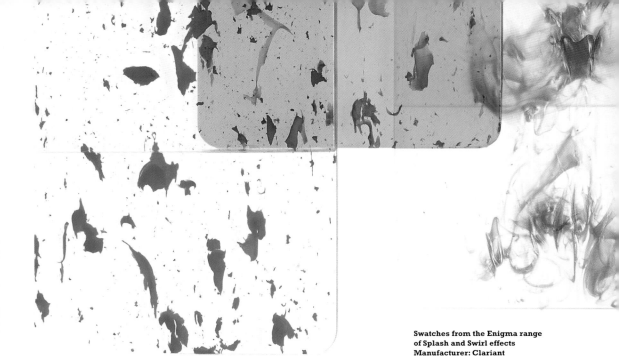

Swatches from the Enigma range
of Splash and Swirl effects
Manufacturer: Clariant

Splashtastic

Dimensions	**Swatch size 400x450mm**
Features	**Unique visual effect**
	Decoration is embedded into the surface, which eliminates the possibility of colors being worn or scratched off
More	**www.clariant.masterbatches.com**
Applications	**The effect can be incorporated into a range of plastic materials, including HDPE, PET, polystyrene, polypropylene, PVC, and SAN. For fashion accessories, these splodge effects can be seen as a competitor to the marbled, cloudy effects of cellulose acetate. Other potential applications include cosmetics packaging.**

The potential of masterbatches—concentrated additives for modifying and coloring plastics—is enormous. They carry out the task of giving plastic resins enhanced features, whether those features are performance-related or, as in this case, purely aesthetic.

Clariant is one of the world's leading producers of masterbatches. Along with scented, chromed, transparent, and other effects, one of Clariant's most unusual products is a decorative effect called Splash.

This special-effect concentrate uses different colored particles that are blended together in a clear or colored base resin to form a series of smudges in the molded component. This means that specific effects can be created at the same time as the molding process, including Tortoiseshell, Mosaic, Smoky Granite, and Graffiti.

Although masterbatches can be added to a whole range of plastic-processing methods, this particular effect is restricted to any injection- or blow-molded component or conversion into sheet form. These effects may not be radical in themselves, but they are new to mass production, capturing a sense of fun and celebration of color.

016

Material becomes surface

PressLoad, made by Cellbond Composites, uses a clever surface design to create a valuable combination of strength, energy absorption, and lightness.

Based on the same principle as an egg box, this is a semi-formed material, born out of technical innovation and designed for a robust engineering use. It also happens to be a fascinating material visually. Originally developed as a lightweight energy absorber to compete with honeycomb and other panel products, PressLoad is more of an innovation as a surface than as a material.

There is a range of different geometries and materials according to application. Beyond thermoset and thermoformed plastics, which include polypropylene and polycarbonate, the principle of this surface can also be used in aluminum alloys. Although the standard form is a sheet, PressLoad can also be formed into curves, where it performs well as an impact absorber.

Features	**Exceptional flexibility when sandwiched**
	Excellent energy absorption
	Cost-effective
	Low cost, high production rates
	Recyclable
More	**www.cellbond.com**
Applications	**This structural panel has uses in aerospace, architectural, marine, and automotive industries. It can be used for ceiling and roof panels in the rail and automotive industry, in the manufacture of hoods and fenders in cars, as decorative panels in the retail and home environments, for raised floors, interior and exterior cladding, and for room dividers. It can also be used for impact protection in transport, and in exhibition stands and decorative panels.**

018

Clear polypropylene
jewel cases

Total clarity

Dimensions	**142x124mm**
Features	**High clarity**
	Cost-effective
	Ability to incorporate live hinges
	Widely available
	Low density
	Good chemical resistance
	Good strength and rigidity
	Recyclable
More	**www.clearpp.com; www.milliken.com**
Applications	**Food and nonfood packaging, centrifugal tubes, disposable syringes for the medical industry, blow-molded bottles.**

When polypropylene (PP) was first introduced, it ushered in a new area of possibilities for plastic products, including live hinges, cost-effectiveness, and toughness. What it lacked, however, was the ability to be completely transparent, having a slight milky haze. When polypropylene is seen alone, this milkiness is not very evident, but when viewed next to a piece of PET (polyethylene terephthalate), it is obvious which one is transparent.

Milliken has a rich history of technical innovation, and since the 1980s it has been developing clarifying agents to overcome this problem with PP. Its latest generation of clear polypropylene should help it compete more with the likes of crystal-clear PET.

**Collar from a perfume
cap provided by DuPont
functional aesthetics**

Sublime color

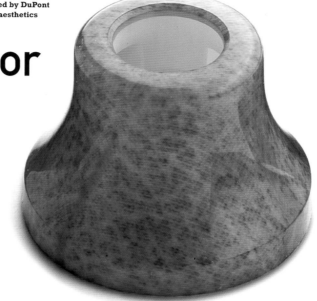

There are several methods of applying decoration and color to plastics once they have been molded. Although used for some time in the textile industry and other two-dimensional print applications, sublimation coating or painting is a new technology for surface decorating in three-dimensional plastic moldings.

Applied as a secondary process after molding, the process works by heating up the printed image or effect and vaporizing it so that it is absorbed onto the substrate. It can be used on a range of materials, with the only restriction being that the substrate is able to withstand the temperature of the process.

The sublimation coating is more than just a skin: the process embeds the pattern between 20 and 30 microns into the surface of the plastic, allowing for components to take on a variety of colors, images, and decorative effects. Because the dyes penetrate the surface of the plastic, the decoration is much more resistant to wear than other techniques, such as in-mold decoration.

The process can be used to decorate and personalize standard products without the need to retool, which can be useful for seasonal and fashion-led products such as skis, where colors or images with exceptional resistance to wear can be applied to existing tooled designs.

Dimensions	**40mm diameter**
Features	**Excellent scratch and wear resistance**
	High resolution
	Can be applied to a range of materials including nonplastics
	Can be used to decorate large-scale moldings
	Easy to customize parts and provide customer differentiation without retooling
	Can be applied to small- or large-scale production
More	**www.kolorfusion.com**
	www.functionalaesthetics.plastics.dupont.com
Applications	**Sporting goods, consumer appliances, and electronics, where a permanent wear-resistant image is required onto a molded piece. Can be applied to a range of different materials, even on a very large scale.**

020

Form-dictated patterns

**Flowerpot showing the effect of
injection-molding surface effects
Designer: Addmix
Manufacturer: Addmix**

The greatness of plastic is the fact that each component that comes out of the machine looks exactly the same with a high degree of technical skill ensuring this uniformity. What is particularly interesting with the intervention in the injection-molding process shown in this particular example is not just the fact that it brings a new possibility to the surface decoration of plastics, but that this marbling effect is a direct result of the form of the molded product.

Add Mix has developed a "dosing" process, where, using virtually any type of granular material, the process of adding different colors during injection molding offers a way of producing plastic components where the surface decoration can be controlled to give different swirling effects.

The nature of these effects is the result of the flow of plastics into the cavity of the tool. Therefore, a simple shape such as a flowerpot will have a very different pattern to a more complex part with more junctions and joints. Nevertheless, because the flow of material is the same each time, the patterns can be reproduced as multiples, no matter how complicated they are.

Dimensions	**220x200mm diameter**
Features	**Distinctive visual quality**
	Existing mold
	Existing machines
	Add-on to different molding machines
	No size limitations
	Can use existing tooling to create something unique
	Can be used for performs for blow moldings
More	**www.addmix.com**
Applications	**Cosmetics, jewelry, fashion accessories, and garden furniture, where it offers a pattern similar to ceramic glazing.**

Metal skins

Think of the door handles on the inside of a car, with sleek, semi-organic contours, or the caps on perfume bottles. These accessories may appear to be metal, but in many cases are merely plastic moldings with a thick, hard, protective metallic skin. This is a technology that is partly concerned with perception of products, but also the practical side of product manufacturing and assembly. Delrin® acetal resins and other engineering polymers have traditionally been difficult to metalize, and although it is possible to injection-mold metals, it incurs higher costs than plastic injection molding.

Metalizing plastics is not particularly new technology, having been used on materials such as ABS for some time. However, what is new is their use on engineering polymers. This allows products to get one step closer not only to replicating the surface of metal, but also to some of the mechanical properties of metals.

Apart from aesthetics, one of the commercial uses for this type of plating allows for a single engineering polymer to replace applications that might have required two components. A perfume cap, for example, would traditionally be made from two moldings—a metal-plated ABS outer cover over a chemically resistant acetyl resin. This new process allows the product to be made from a single engineering component that can be plated.

The technology means that just by looking at a product it would be impossible to know that the substrate was plastic. It is also another example of plastics encroaching on the territory of other materials, using surface as a way to combine the processing of one material with the functional and decorative surface of another.

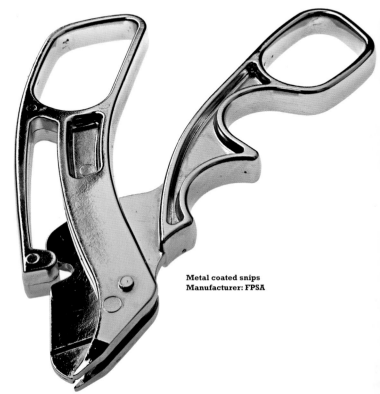

Metal coated snips
Manufacturer: FPSA

Features	Allows for engineering polymers to be plated
	Decorative
	Corrosion resistant
	Wear resistant
	Hard
	Can be cost-effective due to the reduction in the number of components
More	www.functionalaesthetics.plastics.dupont.com
Applications	Door handles in cars, plating in the medical industry, perfume packaging that requires a high level of decoration combined with chemical resistance.

Polar S810i heart rate monitor
Manufacturer: Polar

Adventures in film

There are two noteworthy aspects to in-mold decoration using plastic films. The first is the process, in which the films are used as functional and decorative elements for enhancing molded plastic products. This allows for these printed films to be applied to molded parts during the forming process—a cost-effective method for applying a range of skins to components without secondary processing. The second aspect is to do with the films themselves.

Autotype is a leading company in the production of in-mold decorating films. Two of its most interesting films rely on some fantastic technology. The first is Autoflex MARAG™ (Motheye AntiReflection and AntiGlare). Using nanotechnology, this film replicates the eye structure of a moth, which collects as much light as possible but eliminates any reflection that might attract predators. This phenomenon has been converted into a single-layer film that has the advantage of increasing perceived brightness on a range of portable LCD displays without compromising either the viewing angle or clarity of the screen.

Another interesting product is Autoflex HiForm-M, a polycarbonate film that has the ability to self-heal, repairing itself of minor scratches. The surface of the film is continually moving, which results in the scratches disappearing within 24 hours.

Features	**Allows for virtually any pattern to be added as a skin**
	Easy to customize products without retooling
	High and low production runs
	A range of films are available that are scratch, chemical, and abrasion resistant
	Cost-effective as it is part of the production cycle
More	**www.autotype.com**
Applications	**Cellphone lenses (which exploit the scratch-resistant film), cases and keypads, electronic and flat-panel displays, membrane touch-switches, and interior and exterior automotive accessories.**

All join together

Features	**Chemically dissimilar materials can be joined**
	Permanent bond; Clean technology
	Cost-saving
	Less complex than traditional mechanical joints, such as glue, screws, or welding
	Dissimilar materials can be separated and recycled
More	**www.dupont.com**
Applications	**This technology is still in its early stages, but the potential for joining dissimilar materials opens new doors to material combinations that have previously been difficult or expensive. Costs can be reduced when a part does not have to use a single expensive material when a second cheaper alternative can be used. The process also allows for hard and soft materials to be combined economically.**

The world of fixings deserves a book all to itself, as there are thousands of combinations of materials, adhesives, mechanical fasteners, and welding. Advice on joining similar materials can be quite easy to obtain, but information on joining dissimilar materials can be much harder to find (and understand). For example, engineering polymers are difficult to join because of their excellent chemical resistance.

"Micromechanical anchoring" is a method of joining any two differing materials, including engineering polymers. The process was developed by DuPont. The project began as an investigation into how to join polyethylene (PE) and polyoxymethylene (POM) in fuel containers—a process previously achieved by welding. Researchers came up with a new process to join not only these two materials, but any two materials. It involves overmolding a porous interface sheet of plastic onto a plastic component. This component is then placed into a molding tool, where a second component in a different material can be overmolded. The porosity of the sheet allows the melted material to flow into the pores to give a gripping effect similar to Velcro®.

This process relies on a mechanical effect rather than a chemical interface, and has a continuous in use temperature limitation of 140°F (60°C)—above this, the film is open to attack. This can be an advantage as components can be separated for recycling. The main restriction of the technology is that at least two of the components must be overmolded with the film.

024

Scents and sensibilities

Although the ability to add additional smell to plastics has been around for some time, it has yet to make a significant impact on products. This is partly due to the fact that until recently the scents have only been superficial and have eventually rubbed off, but it may also be due to the fact that most of the smells designed by the various manufacturers have shared a similar, sweetly artificial fragrance.

The automotive industry is one area where the smell of materials is important, as it has to be considered in the design of the confined, personal space of a vehicle's interior.

As technology has progressed to allow us to add long-lasting smells to plastic products through additives in a masterbatch, then perhaps the day will come when brand owners start to embody their brand in a truly evocative or memorable scent. Of course, the challenge lies in creating scents that do not put people off mass-market products, so it may be that scent becomes the main attraction of a given plastic product rather than a perhaps controversial addition to something familiar.

Features	Scents can be incorporated into moldings as an additive
	Scents can last for up to 20 years
	Cost-efficient
More	www.eastmaninnovationlab.com
	www.masterbatches.com
	www.thebrewery-london.com
Applications	Novelty items and stationery.

Scented Pebbles
Designer: The Brewery
Client: Eastman Chemicals

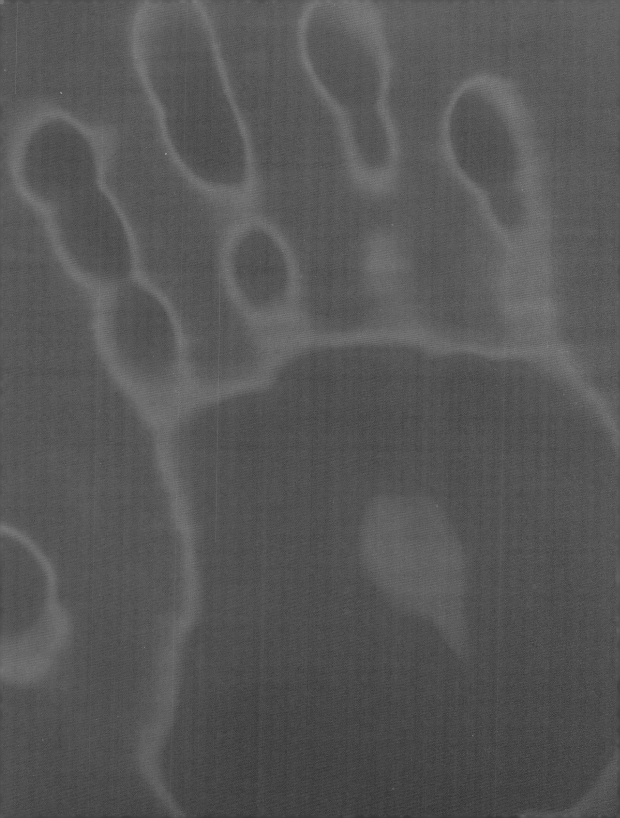

Thermochromic sheet
Manufacturer: Clariant

Invisible made visible

The interesting aspect of any type of thermochromic technology is that it makes visible that which is inherently invisible. It can take the warmth from your hand, for example, and convert it into a series of colors, thereby providing a new way of seeing our environment.

This type of color-changing technology can take various forms. Liquid-crystal thermochromics, for example, are based on the coding of different temperatures into a series of colors. This is the technology behind forehead thermometers, where the change in temperature is reflected by a different color.

ChromaZone is a unique company in that it can supply anything from the initial powder and ink to a semi-finished thermochromic sheet or a finished thermometer. One particularly interesting product that the company produces is a heat-sensing ink in the form of a crayon.

Features	**Can be used in a variety of forms**
	Reversible or nonreversible
	Can be printed or molded
	High visual appeal
	Good safety potential; Fun
More	**www.chromazone.co.uk**
Applications	**Thermochromics can be used in sheet form, printable form, and as a masterbatch additive to a molded product. They are used in children's products, industrial safety signage, promotional products, sunglasses, packaging for batteries, novelty products, mood rings, and food packaging.**

Unrippable

Welcome to the most exciting envelope material ever: a plastic that can be printed, glued, sewn, and, when you have finished with it, can be recycled and converted to car parts, underground cables, and blown film!

Tyvek® is an HDPE (high-density polyethylene fiber)—a plastic that thinks it's a paper. If you don't know this brand by name, you will know it by the waxy, paper-thin, plastic sheet that is used to make virtually unrippable courier envelopes. The texture of the material is the result of the strands of polyethylene in its cross-linked structure.

TYVEK® is produced in three different types: 10, 14, and 16. The fibers in Type 10 style are bonded to form a tough, dense, opaque sheet. The dense packing of the fine, interconnected fibers produces a smooth surface, high opacity, and whiteness. The large number of bonds per unit area results in a stable and abrasion-resistant surface with a stiffness similar to paper. Fiber bonding of Types 14 and 16 is restricted to discrete points in the nonwoven sheet. This produces a high degree of fiber mobility, and gives the non-woven sheet a fabric-like drape.

Tyvek® behaves like any paper product: you can write on it using pencil or pen, pencil marks can be rubbed out, it will not tear at folds, and it can be folded 20,000 times without wearing out. It even floats. When a hole is punched in it, it doesn't weaken the material. Tyvek® is printable by most common techniques (except hot laser and photocopying), and can be printed on most computer printers.

Features	**Super strong; Lightweight**
	Good liquid hold-out characteristics
	Strong and tear resistant
	Weather resistant
	Resists continuous folding and flexing
	Keeps properties across a wide range of temperatures
	Unaffected by most chemicals
	Nontoxic; Chemically inert
	Conforms to International Maritime Dangerous Goods labeling code (also BS-5609)
	Approved for contact with foodstuffs and cosmetics
	Conforms to draft EC directives on packaging waste and German legislation on compatible labeling
More	**www.duponttyvek.com**
Applications	**Security envelopes, protective apparel, specialty packaging, roofing membranes, tags and labels, banners, maps, money, reinforcement, kites.**

Slippery customers

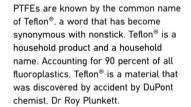

PTFEs are known by the common name of Teflon®, a word that has become synonymous with nonstick. Teflon® is a household product and a household name. Accounting for 90 percent of all fluoroplastics, Teflon® is a material that was discovered by accident by DuPont chemist, Dr Roy Plunkett.

Teflon® is smooth and slippery to the touch. It is heat resistant up to 260 degrees and is available as a sheet, film, thread, tubing, and rod. Grades can be produced to allow it to be created by a number of different processes, including injection and compression molding and extrusion. More famously, it can also be used as a protective covering.

Features	Astonishing chemical resistance
	Excellent mechanical strength
	Self-lubricating
	Low friction coefficient
	Excellent electrical insulation properties
	Maintains properties through a range of temperatures
	Good UV and weather resistance
	Transparent
More	www.dupont.com/teflon
Applications	Bearings, gear wheels, surgical prosthetics, coating for cookware, washers, electrical sleeving, cake tins, stain repellent for fabrics and textile products, tubing and piping in the semiconductor industry, anticorrosion surface coatings.

033 Big

034

Dimensions	**810x1,080x960mm**
Features	**Excellent resistance to chemicals**
	Well balanced relationship between stiffness, impact strength, and resistance
	Colorfast; Low moisture permeability
	Easy to process; Low cost; Recyclable
More	**www.marc-newson.com, www.rotomoulding.org**
	www.excelsior-roto-mould.co.uk
Applications	**Chemical drums, carrier bags, flexible toys, car fuel tanks, cable insulation, furniture.**

Plastic Orgone chair
Manufacturer: Metroplast
Designer: Marc Newson

"I wanted to produce my own inexpensive version of the Orgone chair. We used rotational molding so we could make it relatively cheaply and it sold pretty well."

Marc Newson's emphasis on negative space, which was explored in the original Aluminium Orgone chair, required a manufacturing process that was able to produce hollow forms while using relatively low tooling costs. Due to the nature of rotational molding the chair comes out from the mold as a completely enclosed shape. To obtain the open ends at the top and bottom of the chair requires a degree of post-formed finishing. This involves cutting the ends of the chair off, which is made easier by having a detail of a thin wall section in the mold at the point where it is cut.

Materials used for rotational molding are generally low- or medium-density polyethylenes. Polypropylene is used occasionally where high operating temperatures are required in the final product. Polyamides are also used in specific situations, but due to the high cost are not a common choice.

Hollow forms

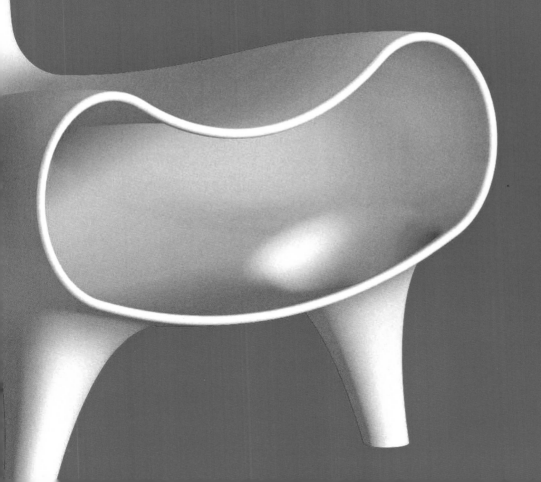

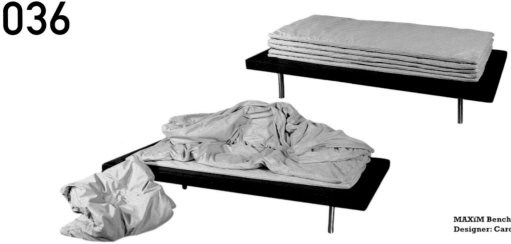

MAXiM Bench
Designer: Caroline Froment

Think of sand

Inspired by the way people on the beach build their rest area in the sand, Caroline Froment designed a piece of domestic furniture that recreates the sensation. The main driving force behind this idea was to find a material that would create the desired effect.

The MAXiM Bench feels quite different to a regular beanbag chair. While both are for sitting, the MAXiM Bench offers much more support to the user's form, as it is filled with millions of micro balloons. In the case of a beanbag chair, the tiny Styrofoam (polystyrene) pellets essentially roll on top of each other and by doing so, do not afford the stability and therefore the comfort of the MAXiM Bench. Not only does the bench conform to the contours of the user, it also allows the user to manipulate the cushions to suit his/her needs. Unlike the beanbag chair, it will retain its new form until someone decides to modify it.

Dimensions	Platform: 2,000x1,000x70mm
	Cushions: 1,800x800x50mm
Features	Low density
	Excellent fluidity
	Nonabrasive
	Small (each sphere 0.5mm diameter)
Applications	In a glass form the micro balloons are used as fillers for various applications to reduce weight. As the micro balloons were designed specifically for the MAXiM there are no other current applications.

Dimensions	**400x150x150mm deflated**
	730x470x420mm inflated
Features	**Good chemical resistance**
	Economical production of large parts
	Good strength and dimensional stability
	No tooling costs
	Good accuracy of mold surface detail
	Easy to combine with other materials
	Excellent surface finish; Recyclable
More	**www.bayer.co.uk, www.via.asso.fr**
Applications	**Medical equipment, furniture, windows, snow boards, decorative moldings.**

Self-assembly

François Azambourg's work is based on ongoing research into new materials and technologies and their application into furniture. The chair is specifically for selling by mail order and through hypermarkets and was inspired by the six-packs of bottles available from supermarkets.

Polyurethanes are important plastics as they can be manufactured in many forms, making them an ideal choice for designers. The Pack chair is fabricated with an internal airtight polyester cloth pouch and a double lining that contains a two-part liquid polyurethane foam. When the user activates a switch the parts are released enabling them to mix together, thereby combusting and filling the form to produce the erect chair. Within a few seconds the form is rigid.

Pack chair
Designer: François
Azambourg

038

Flexible, deformable, exchangeable

Dimensions	**2,500x1,510mm**
Features	**Low weight compared with steel**
	Good color retention; UV stability
	Good impact stength; Corrosion resistant
	Good electrical properties; Chemical resistant
	High-temperature performance; Weathers well
	Flame retardant; Molds quickly
	Very good balance of chemical and mechanical properties
	Low temperature impact strength
	Heat resistance: RTI up to 284°F (140°C)
More	**www.geplastics.com/resins/materials/xenoy.html**
	www.smart.com, www.thesmart.co.uk
Applications	**Automotive fenders and body panels, business equipment housings, cellphone casings, large structural parts.**

The innovative car panels used for the Smart car don't need painting, and will flex so they don't easily dent. The panels are made from XENOY®, an engineering resin created by GE Plastics.

The car, jointly developed by Daimler Chrysler and Swatch, won the Grand Award from the Society of Plastics Engineers in the category of Most Innovative Use of Plastics. The Smart car was born out of a desire to push the car beyond its traditional ideas into new functions, and to look at "the life of materials from factory, through the car's life, to recycling."

The lightweight alternative to steel means that the nine body panels can be fitted more easily, making production simpler, faster, and more cost-effective. The panels are naturally corrosion resistant and a low-impact collision will not dent the car. Each of the panels comes in a wide range of colors and can be changed in less than 30 minutes.

Smart City-Coupé
Daimler Chrysler
Designer: MCC Smart

040

Oz
Client: Zanussi
Designer: Roberto Pezzetta

Refrigerators are mostly made from an outside metal panel with a vacuum-molded internal shell with foam used as an insulatator. Oz breaks the mold of conventional cube fridges. For this new form to be realized a new material needed to be explored. Polyurethane, one of the most important polymers, is available as thermosets and thermoplastics with a wide range of properties from open-cell and crushable foams to closed-cell rigid forms. Oz is made from a flame-retardant Bayer-grade polyurethane, Baydur 110, a rigid integral skin foam. The foams are produced by the release of two chemical components into a mold where they expand and fill the mold, solidifying on contact with the walls. Both the internal and external structures are made from the same material making recycling much simpler.

Foam fridge

Dimensions	1,420x620x420mm
	Door weight: 8.5kg; cabinet weight: 17kg
Features	Economical production of large parts
	Relatively low tooling costs
	Can offer variable wall thicknesses from 3–25mm
	Good strength and dimensional stability
	Good chemical resistance; Easy to paint
	Wide variety of applications and physical properties
	Good accuracy of mold surface detail
	Easy to combine with other materials
	Excellent surface finish; Can be recycled
	Stays rigid even in the lowest temperatures
More	www.zanussi.com, www.bayer.com
Applications	Medical equipment, housing for games and vending machines, furniture, windows, armrests on office furniture, decorative moldings, sports equipment, car instrument panels, fenders, knee pads.

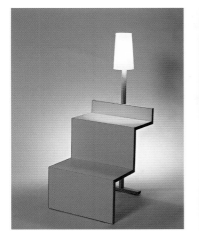

**Wee Willie Winkie
Designers: Dominic Jones
and Chris Lefteri**

Surface as toy

Abet Laminate is a leading manufacturer of high-pressure laminates. The company's priority is the design of the surface, and Wee Willie Winkie is a surface that offers an experience.

The main feature of Wee Willie Winkie is the use of Lumifos, a fluorescent laminate that is glued to an MDF structure. The Lumifos surface has two main functions: the first is to provide a reassuring glow for the child as it sleeps and the second is to provide a surface which the child can play with, creating shadows when objects are placed upon it when the light is turned off.

The aim of this project was to show how a design process could be used to create new forms, utilize new alternative materials, and create new yet relevant scenarios for furniture and products.

Dimensions	**500x500x1,100mm**
Features	**Low cost; Versatile production**
	Good resistance to chemicals
	High surface hardness and scratch resistance
	Good dimensional stability
	Excellent mechanical strength and stiffness
	Excellent reaction to fire, producing low fumes
	Easy to clean; Good water resistance
	Wide range of finishes, colors, and effects
More	**www.abet-laminati.it**
	www.designlaminates.co.nz/abetlaminati.htm
Applications	**Wall cladding, furniture, flooring, work surfaces, door panels.**

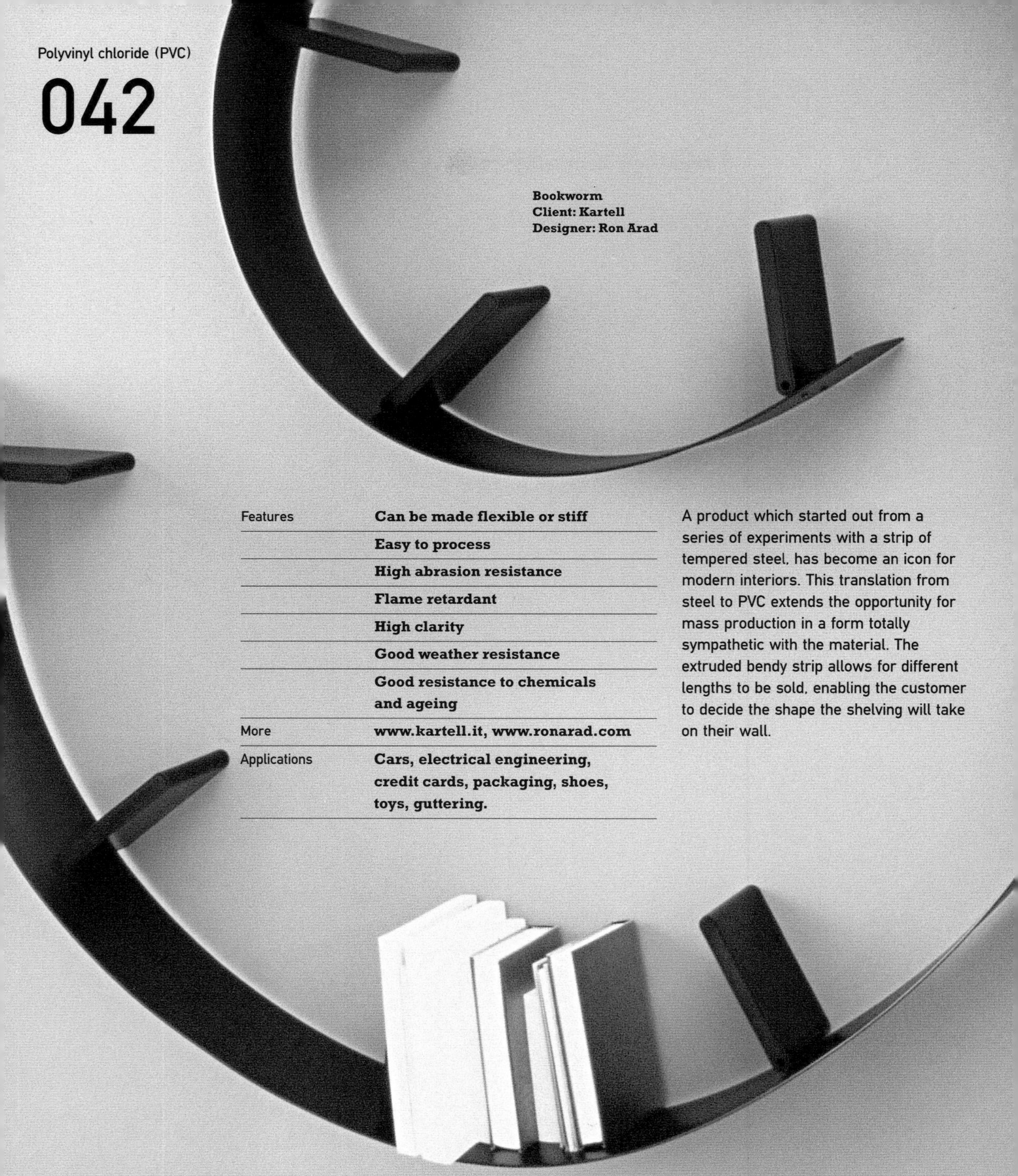

Bookworm
Client: Kartell
Designer: Ron Arad

Features	Can be made flexible or stiff
	Easy to process
	High abrasion resistance
	Flame retardant
	High clarity
	Good weather resistance
	Good resistance to chemicals and ageing
More	www.kartell.it, www.ronarad.com
Applications	Cars, electrical engineering, credit cards, packaging, shoes, toys, guttering.

A product which started out from a series of experiments with a strip of tempered steel, has become an icon for modern interiors. This translation from steel to PVC extends the opportunity for mass production in a form totally sympathetic with the material. The extruded bendy strip allows for different lengths to be sold, enabling the customer to decide the shape the shelving will take on their wall.

Sold by the foot

FPE (Fantastic Plastic Elastic)
Client: Kartell
Designer: Ron Arad

Two flat pieces

Polypropylene raises its head again in the form of a glossy, bendy chair. This chair was originally created for an Adidas Sport Cafe in France. It has a soft and sinuous form. However, this is not only a design shouting a great form but also a product that reflects new production methods for a chair. It is made from only two main components, an extruded aluminum frame and a polypropylene seat. The seat is produced as an injection-molded flat sheet which slots into the frame. This process is completed while the frame is still straight. The whole unit is then put into a press which bends the flat shape into a three-dimensional form. The 5mm-thick polypropylene is a flexible material, which provides a strong joint at the point of contact with the frame. It comes in a range of translucent colors.

Dimensions	**400x780x550mm**
Features	**Good range of translucency and colors**
	Flexible; Excellent live-hinge potential
	Easy and versatile to process
	Excellent resistance to chemicals
	Low density; High heat resistance
	Low water absorption and permeability to water vapor; Recyclable
More	**www.ronarad.com, www.basall.com**
	www.dsm.com/dpp/mepp
	www.dow.com/polypro/index.htm
Applications	**Packaging, domestic accessories, stationery, garden furniture, toothpaste tube lids.**

Amazonia Vase
Client: fish
Designer: Gaetano Pesce

Although he studied architecture and industrial design, Gaetano Pesce's work has explored not just the standardization of mass production but also the notion of the plastic item being unique. His experimentation with furniture began in the 1960s with work for the Italian furniture producer Cassina. One of the recurrent themes in his work is the exploration of interaction between products and their users. In order to reflect this, he has developed a range of products that are deliberately unique.

The originality in his approach comes from his attempt to destroy the idea that plastic products can only be produced by machines where the main criteria are that they are all exactly the same.

Dimensions	**3,530x2,650mm**
Features	**Excellent control; Low tooling cost**
	Allows careful control of color and transparency
	Allows for casting of any thickness
	Perfect clarity; Good adhesive properties
	Versatile forming process
Applications	**Furniture, interiors, sculpture, model making.**

Celebration of chance

Future ideas

Today, most cars are made up of at least 30 different types of plastic, generally making up about 30 percent of all components. The Baja is a lightweight, all-terrain vehicle, one of only two all-plastic cars in production. As such it challenges traditional preconceptions of the use of materials within the automotive industry and demonstrates key advantages over traditional metal alloys.

The Baja is comprised of both thermoset and thermoplastic resins. The body panels are thermoplastic and formed from extruded Korad®, ASA, and ABS vacuum-formed sheet. A composite chassis tub and roof structure are made of stitch-bonded fiberglass, vinylester resin, and a balsa core.

More

www.plastics-car.com/spotlight/
spotlight.htm

www.automotivecomposites.com

Baja
Client: Brock Vinton
Designer: Michael Van
Steenburg, Automotive
Design & Composites Ltd.

Features	Exceptional toughness even at low and high temperatures
	Water-clear transparency
	Unmatched impact resistance
	Good dimensional stability; Flame resistant
	Easy to process; UV stable
More	www.Kartell.it, www.teijinkasei.com
	www.dsmep.com, www.geplastics.com
Applications	Eyewear, water bottles, CDs, DVDs, kitchen containers, business equipment, electrical appliances, glazing, cellphone casings, safety goggles, helmets.

Fashionable toughness

Polycarbonate is a contemporary material used here in the interpretation of an archetypal object and form. The design makes a direct reference to the kind of wooden ladder you might find under the stairs in your grandmother's house. Instead of wood, it uses a modern material which is totally appropriate for this function. Polycarbonate is as tough as polymers come, but is also lightweight and can be produced in a range of colors and finishes.

Polycarbonate's main claim to fame as a polymer is as a super-clear, super-tough material, which is often used as a replacement for glass in glazing applications.

Kartell holds a unique and important role in the field of design. It has been producing domestic objects from plastic since the 1950s. Since then it has pioneered the functional and visual qualities of these materials, creating many well-known and classic pieces of furniture and accessories. As is common with Alberto Meda's work, Upper reflects an understanding of the properties of materials and their application. It is a product that combines the practical, safe, useful, and functional qualities of the material with a seductive, modern, and fashionable aesthetic.

Upper
Client: Kartell
Designers: Alberto Meda
and Paulo Rizzatto

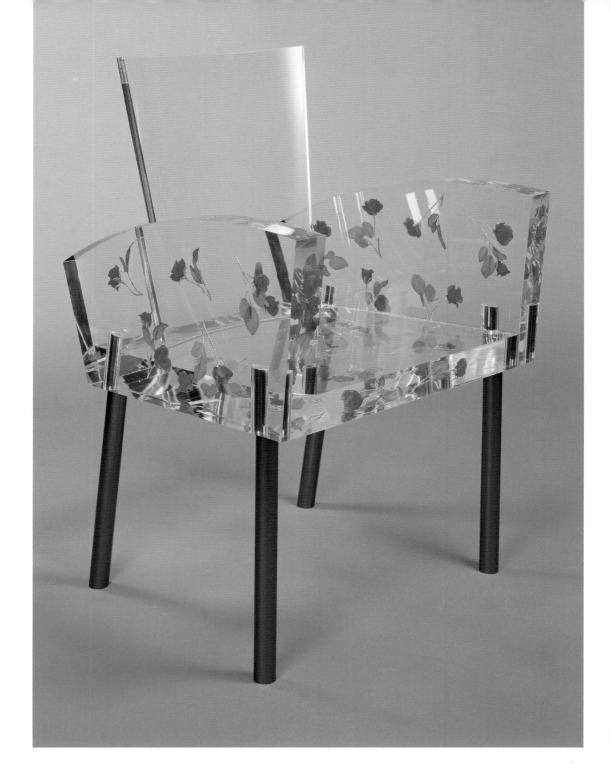

Miss Blanche
Client: Kurumata
Design Office
Designer: Shiro Kurumata

Liquid transparency

Shiro Kurumata has produced many designs where the dominant feature is the element of surprise and the experimental use of materials. This chair was made largely by hand, allowing ultimate control over the design and the aesthetic qualities of the resin. The tooling costs of making the mold were relatively low.

The main body is formed by dropping imitation roses into a mold filled with liquid acrylic resin, which can be done at room temperature. The main technical problem with casting such intricate shapes is the suctioning off of any air bubbles which form around the folds of the petals which are held in place by tweezers. The chair is formed of three separate elements—seat, back, armrests—and once these have cured they can be glued together allowing for complete transparency.

Dimensions	**9,050x6,250x6,000mm**
Features	**Low tooling costs**
	Allows careful control of color and transparency
	Allows for casting of any thickness
	Excellent optical clarity
	Good adhesion
	Outstanding UV resistance
	Versatile forming process
More	**www.ineosacrylics.com**
Applications	**Ornamental paperweights, furniture, interiors, sculpture, model making.**

051 Flat

052

Plastic money

Mylar® and Melinex® are two of the most common polyester films. They can be used for a vast range of applications from video and printed circuit boards to laminating ripstop nylon for use on hot air balloons. In the food packaging industry, Melinex® is used as a lid for ready meals which are kept in freezers and are immediately put in an oven, proving that it is dimensionally stable. It can also take printing very well, another advantage for its use in packaging. Melinex® as a printed film for reprographics springs back to a flat sheet even when tightly rolled up and is heat and chemical resistant.

Dimensions	**Available from 12–350 microns**
Features	**Good temperature resistance; Good optical clarity**
	Excellent print capabilities; Recyclable
	Rigid; Good resistance to chemicals
	Excellent strength compared to cellulose acetate film
	Good dimensional stability; Nontoxic
More	**www.dupontteijinfilms.com**
Applications	**Food wrapping, credit cards, labels, substrate for printed circuit boards, x-ray films, motor insulation, wind surfing sails, lids on yogurt pots, protective window film.**

Features	**Extremely pliable; Clear**
	Adheres to any smooth, dry, glossy surface without additional adhesive
	Offers cost-effective protection of products
	Can be modified to allow for printing
	Range of colors available, including metallic
	Available in a range of gauges and finishes
	Can stretch to 150% of its original shape
	Affordable and easy to use
	Available with UV stabilizer for outdoor use
	Easily protects uneven shapes
More	**www.baco.co.uk**
Applications	**Industrial packaging and food wrap.**

Everybody knows that the best thing about plastic wrap is its ability to stick to itself—that satisfying self-supporting grip that happens when you wrap it over your bowl and it clings. Great designers are able to take these common uses and transform them into new functions.

With Thomas Heatherwick's exhibition for the Glasgow Festival of Architecture and Design there is no traditional use of big construction. It just takes the idea of using an existing material and applying it on a unique scale. The gallery space of almost 1,970 square feet (600m²) has a high ceiling supported by cast-iron columns, which support 75 miles (120.7km) of the industrial version of plastic wrap: stretch wrap. The PVC structure achieves three functions: it suspends, wraps, and separates the exhibits. The lighting is achieved through housing in "basic ducting units," contained within the PVC structure.

Strong, stretchy

Identity Crisis
Client: Glasgow Festival
of Architecture and Design
Designer: Thomas
Heatherwick Studio

Polypropylene (PP)

054

Dimensions	**100x300x400mm**
Features	**Good range of translucency and colors**
	Low density
	Good balance between toughness, stiffness, and hardness
	Easy and versatile to process
	Excellent resistance to chemicals and heat
	Excellent live-hinge potential
	Low water absorption and permeability to water vapor; Recyclable
	Low coefficient of friction
	Relatively low cost
More	**www.vtgdoeflex.co.uk**
Applications	**Furniture, packaging, lighting, table mats, point of sale, folders, folio cases.**

Low-cost tooling for batch production

Design is not always restricted to the creation of beautiful forms and functions but often seeks to solve the problems of high unit and tooling costs by avoiding large-scale production runs. The brief asked for a product that had to be manufactured by mass-production methods, with mass-production unit costs, but without mass-production tooling investment and quantities. Initially the client wanted to use melamine as the material for a take-away lunch box, but this was not the most economical option. The alternative, die-cut polypropylene, was being used in every sphere of product design from packaging to lighting and domestic accessories, but its use had not been fully explored through the process of thermoforming.

The box is made from sheets of 1.2mm food-grade thermoformed polypropylene. The thin sheet gained a rigid structure from the curved surfaces in its form and the minimum 3mm lip which runs around the edge of each unit. The material was also ideal because it is recyclable, and the potential for thermoforming with the material meant that tooling costs and unit prices were low in relation to the production volumes.

Bento Box
Mash & Air
Designers: Toni Papaloizou, Chris Lefteri

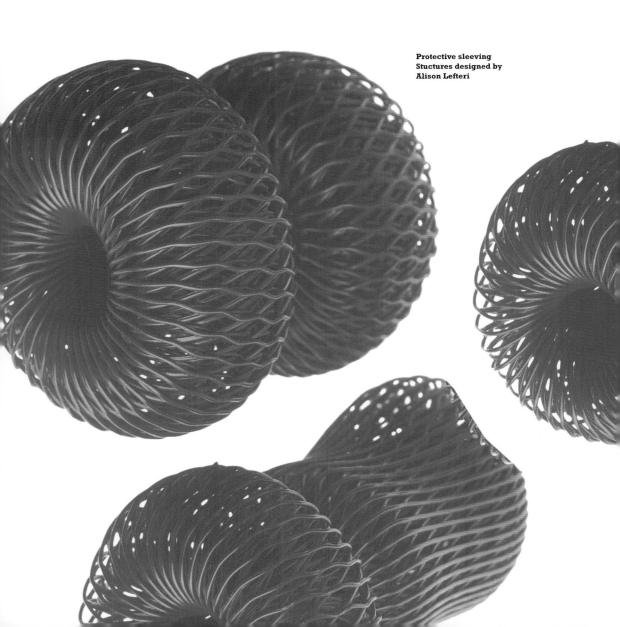

**Protective sleeving
Stuctures designed by
Alison Lefteri**

Flexible and stretchy

Dimensions	**6mm to 400mm diameter tubes**
	Also available in sheet
Features	**Good UV and chemical resistance**
	Strong visual appeal; Easy to color
	Similar to elastomeric materials in flexibility
	Food grade; Formable
	Maintains physical properties at low temperatures
	Contents are exposed but still protected
	Large range of sizes; Good strength-to-weight ratio
More	**www.netlon.co.uk**
Applications	**Packaging, exfoliating scrubs, bra supports, cars.**

This meshy material comes in a wide spectrum of colors and sizes from finger-skinny tubes to super-wide tubes, from soft and flexible to hard, rigid versions. They can be either extruded or woven. EVA is particularly suited for protective packaging because of its natural resistance to chemicals. It can be compared to polyethylene and plasticized PVC. Minimal use of raw material makes it a good economical and environmental alternative to board and molded plastic. It can also be thermoformed giving a whole range of other applications. The open "weave" in the extruded products means that other materials can be formed through and round it.

Acrylic was first developed in the 1930s when its main use was in safety glazing for head gear. It is commonly known as Perspex. The combination of excellent clarity and light weight made it an exciting new plastic. The 1960s saw its applications spread into the domestic environment through its use in contemporary furniture, where new applications were explored by avant-garde furniture designers.

The introduction of a range of colors meant a natural move from lighting into company signage where it is still widely used. Acrylic has a hard surface, which from a distance could easily be mistaken for glass. It is available in both cast and extruded sheet with each being particularly suited to different applications.

Cast sheet is made between sheets of high-quality glass and produced in batches. It has a very high molecular weight making it strong, resilient, and easy to handle and fabricate. The cast method of manufacture is ideally suited to small color runs and batch sizes. Extruded sheet has a lower molecular weight making it easy to vacuum-form and the extrusion process gives excellent thickness tolerance and is economical for long production runs.

Airwave
Bobo Designs
Designers: Tanya Dean,
Nick Gant

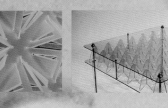

The design of the Airwave table was born out of the nature of Perspex. Its glueless, screwless sheet construction made from 9mm laser-cut components belies its flat origins by forming the illusion of three-dimensional energy and movement when assembled. Perspex's reflective and light-gathering qualities allow it to merge with its environment.

Transparency

Dimensions	**1,000x1,000x450mm**
Features	**High melting point; Low-cost tooling**
	Easy and versatile to fabricate and process
	A wide range of transparent, translucent, and opaque colors and surface finishes
	Laser cutting allows for production of 1 or 100 pieces
	Excellent resistance to chemicals and weathering
	High print adhesion; Fully recyclable
	Excellent optical clarity
	Exceptional color creation and color matching
	Outstanding surface hardness and durability
	An extensive range of sheet sizes and thicknesses
More	**www.ineosacrylic.com, www.perspex.co.uk**
	www.bobodesign.co.uk, www.lucite.com
Applications	**Display, retail signage, furniture, lighting, glazing.**

Abet Laminate has spearheaded innovation with the production of various laminates including Diafos, the first transparent laminate. It has worked with some of the most prominent designers of the twentieth century, and is known for its experimentation with surface. Straticolour is a unique product made by Abet Laminate, which explores the function and visual qualities of edging.

With standard-thickness laminate sheet there are two layers of material. The core is made from layers of paper, which are impregnated with aminoplastic resins, and laid on to that is a surface made of decorative papers impregnated with melamine resins. In Straticolour, Abet has introduced the decorative layer as the core of the material. The edge can be polished giving a unique edging detail.

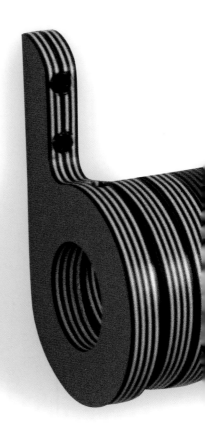

The edge

Dimensions	Standard-size sheets 1,220x3,050mm
Features	High abrasion resistance; High impact resistance
	Excellent moisture resistance; Easily glued
	Good water, chemical, and vapor resistance
	Easy to clean
	Good dimensional stability; Hard wearing
	Highly decorative finish on edges
	Economical compared to other solid surfacing materials
More	www.abet-laminati.it
Applications	Office furniture, interior and exterior paneling, flooring, street furniture, worktops.

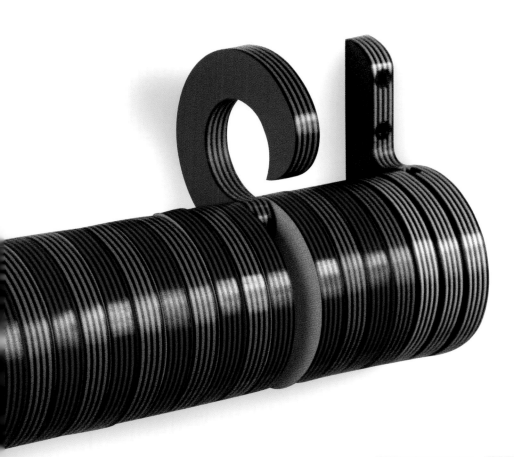

Pianomo (center)
Designer: Shun Ishikawa
Ringo (right)
Designer: Matthew
Jackson
W Table (far right)
Designer: Adrian Tan

062

Works like paper

Dimensions	**30x30x10mm; 10x43x129mm; 1,450x2,000mm**
Features	**Can be heat-welded, ultrasonically welded, riveted, stitched, and embossed**
	Easy to process; Excellent resistance to chemicals
	Excellent live-hinge potential; Recyclable
	Low water absorption and permeability to water vapor
	Manual assembly process; High print adhesion
	Virtually tear resistant; Low density; Cheap tooling
More	**www.vtsdoeflex.co.uk**
Applications	**Furniture and packaging.**

Tummy and Bow Bags (left)
Spine Knapsack (center)
Issey Miyake, Japan
Designer: Karim Rashid
Placemats (right)
Designer: Sebastian Bergne

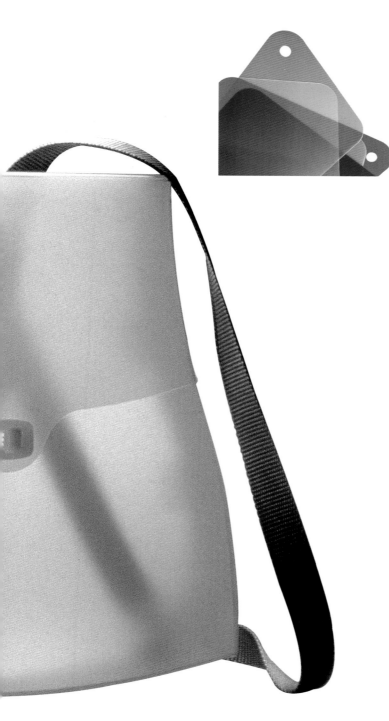

The manufacturer Authentics has had a large impact on the use of molded polypropylene, but an area where it is widely used is as a flat-sheet material. As sheet it has provided the opportunity for plastic products to be made from paper processes like folding, cutting, and creasing with the result that products need minimal investment in tooling. As a result it has become extensively used in all forms of packaging. It needs no tooling to make prototypes, just a sharp knife, a ruler, and a cutting mat.

The Spine Knapsack is one of a series of bags designed exclusively for Issey Miyake boutiques. These sheets of recyclable, extruded, transparent polypropylene have seams (or living hinges) that are easy to flatten down to their two-dimensional shape. The interior has a co-extrusion of fluorescent polypropylene that is reversible, which changes the interior glow of the bag from yellow to orange. The translucent latch is injection-molded polypropylene.

The Tummy and Bow bags, also designed for Issey Miyake, are both created from the same pattern. The garment is placed in the center and the bag is folded and snapped together to create a very rigid and strong package. They stack in three different configurations for store display.

Tailoring in plastic

Colourscape
Client: Colourscape
Music Festival
Artist: Peter Jones

Features	Easy to process with low-cost tooling
	Flexible; Easy to color
	Good transparency; Good UV properties
	Easy for making one-off prototypes
More	www.colourscapefest.in2home.co.uk
	www.oxyvinyls.com
Applications	Cable insulating sheaths, sewage pipes, table cloths, handle grips for bikes, toys, packaging, wallpaper.

The artist Peter Jones uses plastic to explore space and color. His work has been described in many ways—as sculpture, architecture, and even as archisculpture.

Each inflatable structure is composed of a number of primary colored, translucent PVC panels that are positioned to overlap each other and form different color variations and combinations. As visitors walk through the installation the colors appear to change as one panel overlaps another. So strong is this impression that visitors often mistake the effect as being achieved through colored lights. In its pure form PVC is very strong, and, due to the transportation and storage of the structures, this thin 0.25mm material is ideal.

Processing
Sicoblock (right)
Flat-sheet material
(below)
Manufacturer:
Acordis

Dimensions	**630x1,430mm; 6–8mm thickness**
Features	**Low heat and thermal conductivity**
	Distinctive visual appearance; Gloss finish
	Good range of visual effects; Antistatic
	Good electrical insulation properties
	Self-shining; Excellent impact resistance
	Good transparency; Versatile production
	Made from renewable source
More	**www.mazzucchelli1849.it/newsite/inglese /comphist.htm**
Applications	**Safety and sports goggles, frames for sun glasses, jewelry, watch straps, raincoats, lighting, bags.**

Swirling clouds of color inside a warm slice of processed cotton. This distinctive quality is what makes cellulose acetate unique. The process, used to make the flat sheets, has been used since the founding of Mazzucchelli in 1849.

You will need:
• A large amount of cotton plant or wood pulp
• Natural minerals of artificial dye (for color)
• A good quantity of acetate
• A sharp knife
• A large sealable container

Handmade

What to do:
First pick the cotton and through the process of purification produce cellulose. If you don't have cotton you can use wood pulp. Once you have obtained the cellulose, mix it together with acetate and add your own choice of natural mineral or artificial color—the choice of color is obviously up to you. Add plasticizers and light and heat stabilizers as required. Pass this mixture through rollers to obtain a flat sheet, known as the "hyde." The hyde should be a soft, floppy sheet which resembles a leather hyde. Then with your knife cut the hyde into a number of shapes. Carefully lay your cut-out shapes in the large container. Now apply heat and pressure to the container and bury underground. When your mixture has reached the consistency of a thick jelly it is ready to be cut from the block into thin slices. Hang these slices out to dry.

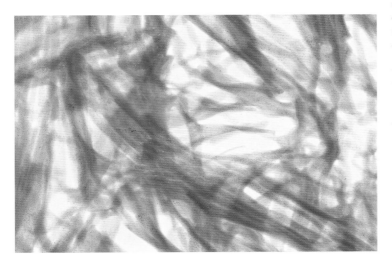

Lighting in a box

Ultra Luz range
Client: Proto Design
Designers: Marco Sousa
Santos, Pedro S. Dias

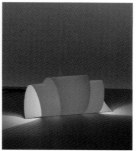

Features	**Nonflammable; Washable; Unbreakable**
	Can be heat welded, ultrasonically welded, riveted, stitched, and embossed
	Excellent resistance to chemicals
	Easy and versatile to process
	Excellent live-hinge potential; High print adhesion
	Low water absorption and permeability to water vapor; Manual assembly process
	Recyclable; Very cheap tooling
More	**www.vtsdoeflex.co.uk**
Applications	**Furniture, packaging, lighting, stationery, table mats, point of sale.**

The Ultra Luz range is the result of a brief to investigate the potential for a self-assembly light which only uses flat polypropylene sheet and standard light fixtures. The restrictions placed on this simple and inexpensive production process forced new approaches to the aesthetics and function of lighting.

Polypropylene sheet offers a range of colors and printing processes that can be used to give this material endless potential to create new forms for everyday products. The collection consists of a range of 19 models of pendant and table lights, which all self-assemble.

Cheap tooling

Features	Easy to process with low-cost tooling
	Flexible and versatile
	Easy to color; Good UV properties
	Easy for making one-off prototypes
	Tough even at low temperatures
	Good transparency
More	www.inflate.co.uk, www.vinylinfo.org
Applications	Chemical drums, carrier bags, toys, car fuel tanks, cable insulation, furniture.

The uses of PVC within manufacturing are extensive, but Inflate has done more to create a fun, dynamic expression of the accessible, cheap qualities of this sheet material and bring it to the forefront of people's attention. Their use of inflatables solved the problem of how to mass-produce in plastics with low-cost tooling and investment. The value of their diverse range of inflatable products comes from the fact that they create original products by restricting the manufacture and production to one material and one process (ultrasonic welding).

Dip molding was a natural evolution of the inflatable products. It fulfilled the criteria of bright colors and cheap, flexible production. Inflate have taken the low-tech principles of PVC sheet and until then, low-value products, and have found new objects with high-value appeal, while still using a very basic process.

Their achievement reverses the perception of plastic as only a high investment material for mass production, with its use here for a "hands on," process with minimal tooling. Products can be just as easily produced as one-offs or in their thousands.

1. Stencil for prototype

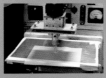

2. Transfer of template

3. Welding machine

Table light
Client: Inflate
Designer: Nick Crosbie

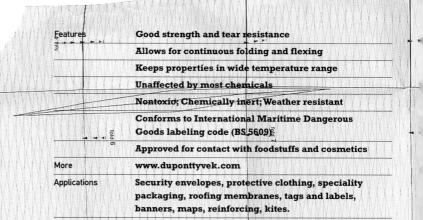

Features	Good strength and tear resistance
	Allows for continuous folding and flexing
	Keeps properties in wide temperature range
	Unaffected by most chemicals
	Nontoxic; Chemically inert; Weather resistant
	Conforms to International Maritime Dangerous Goods labeling code (BS 5609)
	Approved for contact with foodstuffs and cosmetics
More	www.duponttyvek.com
Applications	Security envelopes, protective clothing, speciality packaging, roofing membranes, tags and labels, banners, maps, reinforcing, kites.

Paper thin, super strong

Tyvek® is the DuPont trade name for a range of high-density polyethylene sheet materials. This Hussein Chalayan Tyvek® dress was designed with the intention of igniting the debate about letter writing, and could be regarded as clothing, art, or a letter. It is deliberately constructed to fold and roll in on itself. The size of the garment can be adjusted to fit through use of perforations and adhesive labels.

Airmail dress
Client: Hussein Chalayan
Designers: Rebecca and Mike

By Airmail
Par Avion

072

Dimensions	Sheet size 3,680x760x13mm
Features	Malleable when heated
	High impact resistance
	Strong and hard
	Scratches are easy to remove
	Enables versatile production methods
	Highly workable
	Hygienic; Stain resistant
	Comes in variety of thicknesses as sheet
	Good color-fade resistance
	Excellent resistance to chemicals
More	www.corian.com, www.dupont.com
Applications	Furniture, work surfaces, lighting, retail, intelligent desktops/worktops, transportation, wall cladding, shelving.

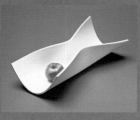

Designer: Gitta Gschwendtner
and Fiona Davidson
Client: DuPont Corian©

Corian® is the trade name for a composite of natural minerals, pure acrylic polymer, and pigments. This homogeneous material was launched as a kitchen worktop material and can be cast, sanded, sandblasted, thermoformed, vacuum-molded, and fabricated into a vast range of shapes and forms. It is inherently strong, durable, and highly workable. It has a hard marble-like surface but is warmer, with a silky-smooth natural finish. Scratches and blemishes can be sanded away and the surface polished. DuPont offer it in a range of 93 colors and textures including translucent and light-reflecting finishes. The fabrication of sheets can be done with minimal tooling, and sheets can be joined by a special two-part adhesive to create an almost seamless joint.

Shapes and recesses can be carved or molded into the surface of the material allowing for new functions in standard desktops. These products rely on the material being heated, restricting the movement of Corian® while it cools through the use of basic wooden jigs and clamps. This simplified manufacturing philosophy results in a range of objects that unashamedly exhibit their sheet material origins.

Out of the kitchen

075 Main Dishes

Heat resistant, flexible

Dimensions	110x210mm
Features	**Excellent outdoor properties**
	Low-cost tooling; Simple processing
	Soft; Forms can have undercuts
	Easy for making one-off prototypes
	Good tactile qualities; Cheap material
More	**www.droog.nl, www.vinylinfo.org**
	www.dmd-products.com
Applications	**Handle-bar grips.**

Droog Design challenges the notion of various object typologies and experiments with changing the preconception of the function of materials. They are not content to merely provide new forms, but seek to create products with new functions and meanings. They reconcile the use of plastic as a high-volume material with freethinking and experimentation, which can result in the production of 10 or 1,000 units of a design.

PVC is an extremely versatile polymer. In its pure state it is a rigid material—it is through the addition of plasticizers that it can become soft as in PVC sheet which was used for the Soft Lamp. Arian Brekveld's light uses a very common dip-molding process to take PVC to new territory. The heat-resistant PVC has the appearance of glass with its translucent quality, allowing enough light through to provide a soft glow when the light is on and also provide a new tactile experience.

Soft Lamp
Client: DMD
Designer: Arian Brekveld

078

Metal to plastic

Dimensions	**200x60x50mm**
Features	**Low cost; Versatile production**
	Good resistance to chemicals
	High surface hardness and scratch resistance
	Good dimensional stability; High impact strength
	Excellent mechanical strength and stiffness
More	**www.acco.com, www.geplastics.com**
Applications	**Consumer electronics, toys, white goods, automotive consoles, door panels, exterior grilles.**

Acco wished to replace its high-volume, cost-effective stapler with an updated and improved design while not increasing the cost. Through thorough analysis and mindful engineering the design team was able to create an ABS stapler that fails less than one percent of the time in extensive performance and testing. The ribs not only contribute visually to the design, but also provide much needed rigidity in the cap helping it to achieve its superior performance. The product can be assembled and disassembled using no tools and can be easily separated for recycling.

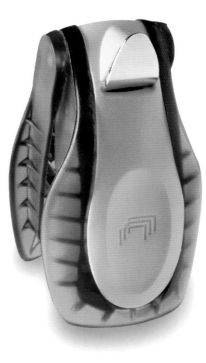

Swingline Desktop/Swingline Worx '99 Mini Staplers
Client: Acco
Designer: Scott Wilson

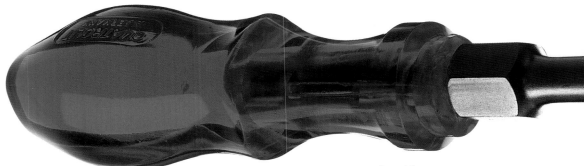

Screwdriver
Acordis

Warm

Features	
	Low heat and thermally conductive
	Flexible production; Good range of visual effects
	Excellent flow properties; Excellent gloss finish
	Good electrical insulation properties
	Antistatic; Self-shining; Good transparency
	Excellent impact resistance
	Distinctive visual appearance
	Made from renewable source
Applications	**Tool handles, hair clips, toys, goggles and visors, spectacle frames, toothbrushes, cutlery handles, combs.**

Warm to the touch, perspiration tolerant, and self-shining, cellulose acetate with its brightly colored transparency is one of the most easily recognizable polymers due to its marbled effect as seen in such items as tool handles and spectacle frames. For its use in hand tools it provides a good compromise between excellent impact resistance and good tactile quality. Other materials like polypropylene have better impact resistance but would probably feel more slippery. The self-shining element comes from the soft nature of the material, and light scratches on its surface can be polished away. Made partly from cotton and wood (cellulose), it can be injection molded, rotationally molded, and extruded. It can also be purchased in sheet form.

Ancient process and modern material

These organic-looking structures have a very unlikely origin. Turned on a lathe using a form of PVC usually used for conduit tube, these pieces use a modern industrially produced preformed material, with a craft process.

The designers are not experimenting with the raw material, but instead use industrial preformed, extruded material intended for other functions and transform these through an intermediary step in another product. The simple angular cuts give unpredictable shapes, providing a semi-solid form. The objects are produced from a variety of solid and tubular PVC parts. The individual tubes are first glued together into a block. Depending on the final shape they are either turned or cut using a band saw. The forms are kept deliberately simple in order to reveal the idea rather than a shape. The tube diameters vary from 50mm to 16mm.

Dimensions	**Largest 250x400mm diameter**
	Smallest 150x300mm diameter
Features	**Excellent resistance to chemicals**
	Good toughness and rigidity
	Can be made stiff and strong
	Easy to process; Relatively low cost
	Good clarity; Good weather resistance
	Flame retardant
More	**www.vinylinfo.org, www.basf.de**
	www.oxyvinyls.com
Applications	**Pipe, guttering, shoes, cable insulation, toys, injection-molded housings for products, extruded panel products, glazing, packaging, credit cards.**

Contenants
Client: Self-initiated project
Designer: Dela Lindo

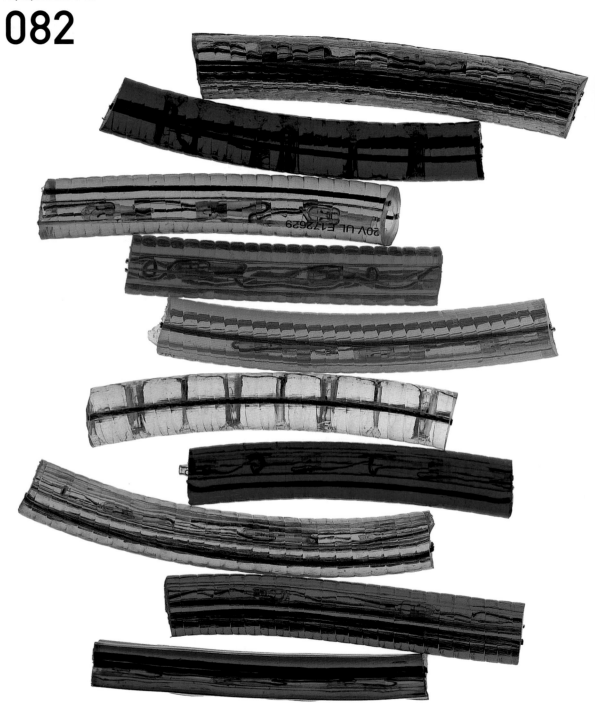

A series of tiny LEDs encapsulated in a flexible tube of light is the principle behind this light fitting. Because the bulbs are sealed within this PVC skin it is impossible to replace them. The miniature bulbs in the Flexilight are made with special Fuse bulbs so that only the defective bulb will go off without affecting the other bulbs in the series.

The light is the perfect application of molded PVC. It is categorized as a commodity plastic, the lowest end of the scale for plastics in terms of cost. It is therefore ideal for this application where large amounts of the material are needed. This fact, combined with the ability of PVC to be altered and added to creating many grades, makes it the natural solution for low-cost consumer products.

Flexilight
Client: Wideloyal
Industries Ltd.

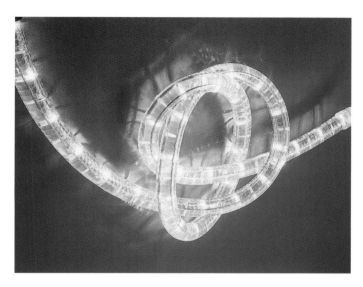

Rope lighting

Features	Additives can give it a large range of properties
	Easy to process; Easy to color
	Versatile
	Good corrosion and stain resistance
	Cost effective; Good rigidity
	Excellent outdoor performance
	Good resistance to chemicals
More	www.wideloyal.com.hk
Applications	Packaging, dip molding, drain pipes, domestic appliances, credit cards, raincoats, car interiors.

Posacenere (Ashtray)
Designer: Anna Castelli Ferrieri
Client: Kartell

It's a heavy, rigid material with the potential for a high-gloss finish. It imparts absolutely no smell or taste to food and feels hard, dense, rigid, and unbreakable. Melamine is from the same family of thermosets as urea-formaldehyde and phenolic resins, although it is more expensive than the other members of the group. The hard, shiny, nonporous surface is partly why it has been a popular alternative to ceramics in the design of dishes, plates, and bowls.

In the 1930s melamine compounds replaced Bakelite due to their ability to absorb and retain a range of colors. The 1950s were the heyday for molded melamine when it was widely used for bright, multicolored tableware products.

Low-volume production

Dimensions	30x130mm diameter
Features	Odor free; Good electrical insulation
	High impact resistance; Stain resistant
	Fire resistant; Heat resistant; Easy to color
	Excellent resistance to chemicals
	Scratch resistant; Very high gloss
	Limited production methods
More	www.perstorp.com, www.kartell.it
Applications	Handles, fan housings, circuit breakers, ashtrays, buttons, dinnerware, laminates.

Today it is available as a compound for molding but is probably used more as a resin for binding paper in plastic laminates. As a raw material it is translucent but the addition of certain fillers, commonly cellulose, can provide greater strength, stability, and easier colorability. In terms of production, it can be injection molded and compression molded, which uses powder and can give a superior finish.

Radius Original Toothbrush
Client: Radius
Designer: James O'Halloran

Tasteless

Until the invention of nylon in the 1930s, bristles for toothbrushes were made from wild boar or horsehair. Cellulose propionate is produced by only one company in the world, Eastman Chemicals. It is one of the very few plastics derived from a renewable source. Used in toothbrushes it offers an alternative to its closest cousin, cellulose acetate, which has a slight sharp taste in the mouth.

Features	**No taste; Warm feel**
	Distinctive visual appearance
	Lightweight; Easy to process
	Good range of visual effects; Good transparency
	Excellent gloss finish; Good elasticity
	Excellent impact resistance
	Made from renewable source
More	**www.radiustoothbrush.com**
	www.eastman.com, www.dupont.com
Applications	**Tool handles, hair clips, toys, goggles and visors, spectacle frames, toothbrushes.**

"Until now the process of making any object could be summarized as one or more of the following:

1. Waste: chip, carve, turn, mill, chisel, i.e. the removal of excess material
2. Mold: injection molding, casting, blow molding and to some degree, extruding, i.e. pouring material as a liquid to take the form of its vessel and then harden
3. Form: bending, pressing, hammering, folding, vacuum forming, i.e. a sheet material forced into a shape
4. Assemble: welding, gluing, bolting, i.e. joining parts together by any means

Now, there is a fifth way—GROW!" says Ron Arad.

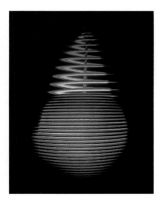

Not Made by Hand
Not Made in China
Distributor: Gallery Morman
Designers: Ron Arad,
Geoff Crowther,
Yuki Tango,
Elliott Howes

The fifth way

All the objects you see in this collection were "grown" in a tank by computer-controlled laser beams; the objects themselves could not possibly have been made by any of the four processes listed above.

Selective Laser Sintering (SLS) technology has traditionally been used by engineers to produce a rapid prototype of a product. The process starts by taking a three-dimensional computer image and sending it to a machine that makes a perfect reproduction of the design. A laser beam is sent through a polyamide powder, which, at selected locations, is hardened into a solid material. Components are built as a series of layers. The fact that the powder is a solid means that parts do not need the supporting struts required for another rapid-prototyping process, stereolithography, that uses a liquid polymer instead of a powder.

Features	Good for working prototypes
	Rough surface that can be improved by post finishing
	Higher cost than stereolithography
	Good for parts that require high mechanical and thermal resistance
	Can produce characteristics comparable to injection-molded parts
More	www.materialise.be
	www.ronarad.com
Applications	Functional products with snap fits, live hinges, thermally and mechanically loaded parts.

088

Surface as brand

The Authentics brand has become synonymous with stony, matte, sorbet-colored translucent plastic. They are known for modern interpretations of utilitarian products that subtly convey functions of modern living.

Authentics has led the way with polypropylene, a fashionable material in both molded and sheet form. The large areas of flat plastic are susceptible to scratches and imperfections which the matte texture can hide. The use of injection molding means that individual products can be produced at a price to suit their purpose. This spoon is designed to allow you to cool hot soups or sauces by passing them from one bowl to the other before drinking.

SIP tasting spoon
Client: Authentics
Designer: Sebastian Bergne

Dimensions	**230x55x15mm**
Features	**High heat resistance**
	Excellent resistance to chemicals
	Low water absorption and permeability to water vapor
	Can be flexed thousands of times without breaking
	Good balance between toughness, stiffness and hardness
	Easy and versatile to process
	Relatively low cost
	Low density; Low coefficient of friction
More	**www.dsm.com/dpp/mepp**
	www.basell.com, www.dow.com/polypro/index
Applications	**Garden furniture, food packaging, bottle crates.**

Acrylonitrile Butadiene Styrene (ABS), a thermoplastic copolymer resin, offers a good balance of properties that can be tailored to suit specific needs. Its main physical properties are its hardness, toughness, and rigidity.

The resin grades of ABS consist of a blend of an elastomeric (rubber) element, which is the polybutadine, providing good impact strength, an amorphous thermoplastic of styrene which gives processing ease (easy flow in the mold), and acrylonite, which helps with hardness, rigidity, and resistance to chemicals. The control of these three monomers gives designers the flexibility needed for the final application. It is probably due to this that it is used widely in domestic appliances and white goods. Although not as tough as some other engineering polymers it offers excellent cost effectiveness.

Inspired by childhood memories, Stefano Giovannoni created this range of plastic products for Alessi. He has allowed the materials to be fully utilized to create brightly colored characters. ABS is used in the hard-wearing application of a can opener, which has a special mechanism that allows for the opened part of the can to be reused as a lid.

Dimensions	**190x65mm**
Features	**High-impact strength even at low temperatures**
	Good stiffness and mechanical strength
	Good scratch resistance; Low specific gravity
	Relative thermal index up to 176°F (80°C)
	Good dimensional stability at high temperatures
	Flame resistant; Easy to process
	Can achieve a high gloss; Easy to match colors
	Cost-effective compared with other thermoplastics
More	**www.alessi.com, www.geplastics.com www.basf.de**
Applications	**Automotive consoles, door panels, exterior grilles, domestic appliance housings.**

Can Can
Client: Alessi
Designer: Stefano Giovannoni

Blended

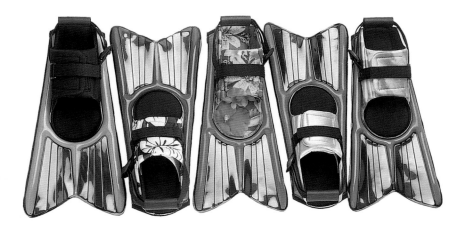

FAB FORCE™
Designer: Bob Evans

TPEs offer the feel of rubber with the processing capabilities of thermoplastics. TPE is a generic term used to describe a family of thermoplastic elastomers which include TPOs (thermoplastic olefins) and TPSs (thermoplastic styrenes). These are all engineering polymers, which offer flexibility and toughness for most conditions. TPEs can generally be molded by injection molding, blow molding, or extruding.

The use of TPEs is perfect for the "snappy blade" characteristics of diving fins. The FAB FORCE™ is manufactured by using low-tech tooling and casting polyurethane in a mold with layers of fabric.

Flip back

Features	**Flexible, Easy to color**
	Available in a range of Shore hardnesses
	Can be extruded, injection molded, and blow molded
	Can be reinforced with glass fiber
	Keeps its properties at low temperatures
	Can be painted; Recyclable
	Good resistance to tearing and abrasion
	Good resistance to weather and seawater
	Good resistance to oil and chemicals
More	**www.forcefin.com**
	www.aestpe.com
	www.basf.com
Applications	**Automotive, mechanical engineering, sports shoes, shock absorbers, side trims for cars, hand tools, ski boots, snow chains**

Use it in the oven

Silicone can take on a multitude of forms and functions; by adding carbon or silver particles to silicone, it can be made to be as conductive as copper wire or an effective insulator. One of the main distinctions silicone has over conventional rubbers is its ability to withstand high temperatures. It also has an ability to be adapted to form different grades, and it feels and looks great.

The W2 products are made from a grade of high-consistency, heat-cured silicone. These home accessories utilize the ability of silicone to be produced in a range of colors, transparencies, and toughnesses. They have a milky translucency (silicone can also be made to be optically clear, photochromic, and fluorescent), but with their soft, squidgy, jelly-like feel they are also interesting to the touch. However, silicone is not limited to accessories in the home—it is even heat-resistant enough to cook bread in.

Features	Large range of possible grades
	Easy to color; Expensive
	Can be made to be optically clear
	Can withstand a wide range of temperatures
	UV resistant; Good tactile qualities
	Food safe; Chemically inert
More	www.w2products.com, www.gesilicones.com
Applications	Electrical encapsulation, tubing, high temperature "O" rings, heat shrinkable tubing, surgical equipment, structural adhesives, baby teats, keypad mats, insulation on power lines, oven door seals, baking trays.

Soapy Joe
Client: W2
Designers: Jackie Piper,
Vicky Whitbread

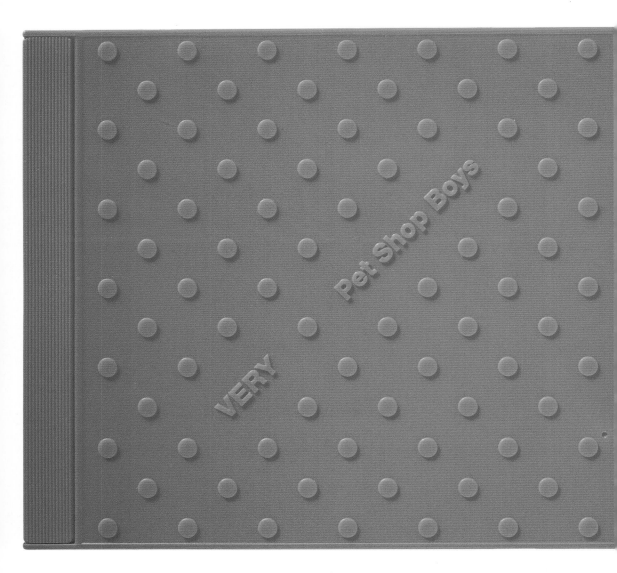

Surface design

Although made from the same material as a conventional jewel case, this product screams out its difference to other CD packaging by featuring a series of orange studs on an orange box. In order to appreciate how much of a departure this product is, you only have to look at how minor the design elements are but how radical the packaging appears. Even the arrangement of the studs is controlled to accommodate the suction pads, which hold the CDs in the case.

Styrol (styrene) was discovered in the middle of the nineteenth century but was not commercially exploited until the 1930s. It is connected with the styrene family which includes ABS, SAN, and SMA ASA copolymers. It is one of the most widely used plastics for a massive range of applications.

Features	**Excellent clarity; Good stiffness**
	Easy to process; Easy to color
	Relatively low cost compared with other polymers; Good transparency
	Very low water moisture absorption
	Easy to mold and process
	Good dimensional stability
More	**www.dow.com/styron/index.htm**
	www.huntsman.com, www.atofina.com
Applications	**Packaging, toys, coat hangers, household and electrical appliances, model kits, disposable cups.**

Very
Client: Parlophone Records
Designer: Daniel Weil

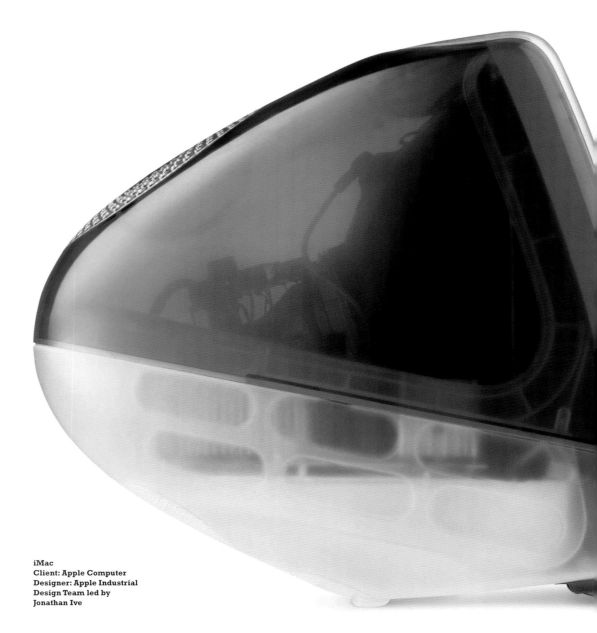

iMac
Client: Apple Computer
Designer: Apple Industrial
Design Team led by
Jonathan Ive

Steamy shower

Apple's statement and reaction against the bland, beige ABS computer boxes needed a new material. It had to provide the opportunity for people to be aware of the technology at the heart of the machine, but without showing too much of the ugly internal workings.

The design team looked at various ways of creating the diffused, translucent, frosty quality. Analogies were made with the effect of a steamy shower, where you don't see everything. The range of candy colors and surface treatments like the ribbed effect exploit the transparency of the casing, the ribs being on the inside to maintain a smooth outer surface. Polycarbonate offers excellent transparency and colorability combined with a very high degree of toughness. The evolution and advancement of the internal technology meant that later graphite models of the iMac could be more transparent as the internal workings became more refined.

Dimensions	**381x381x435mm**
Features	**Excellent range of colors**
	Excellent optical clarity; Easy to process
	Outstanding impact resistance
	Available as transparent, translucent, and opaque
	Excellent dimensional stability, even at high temperatures
	Good heat resistance up to 257°F (125°C)
	Flame resistant; UV stable
	Durable; Recyclable; Nontoxic
More	**www.apple.com, www.geplastics.com**
	www.dsmep.com, www.teijinkasei.com
Applications	**Safety helmets, eyewear, CDs, DVDs, kitchen containers, computer housings, architectural glazing, cellphone housings.**

Will
Client: AOYOSHI Co. Ltd.
Designer: Hiroshi Egawa

Warm it up

Features	Wide variation in forms, physical, and mechanical properties
	Outstanding flex life and cut resistance
	Good abrasion resistance
	High tensile and tear strength
	Good chemical resistance
	High elasticity; Easy to color
More	www.diaplex.co.jp
	www.mediagalaxy.co.jp/aoyoshi/index.htm
Applications	Sheeting, car fenders, bladders, fuel line tubing, packaging material, car body moldings.

099 Commodity Polymers

Bright space Geodesic structure
Designer: Nick Gant
Manufacturer: Bright

Paper-thin buildings

Features	High-impact resistance
	Clarity; Tough
	Chemically resistant; Odor-free
	Cost-effective
	No whitening on fold lines
More	www.bobodesign.co.uk/bright
	www.eastman.com
	www.barloplastics.com
Applications	Signs and displays, which exploit the material's ability to be easily cut, bent—hot or cold—and printed. Spectar® sheet can be routed, welded, drilled, die-punched, or joined by screws, rivets, or bolts. It can also be cut on conventional table, band, or radial-arm saws. It accepts screen-printing, painting, and hot-stamping easily. Even strong cleaning solutions will not affect the material's transparency.

Flat-pack usually implies packaging and furniture made from rigid cardboard, wood, or similarly inflexible materials. The structures designed by Nick Gant for Bright challenge this notion: they are produced from an ultra-thin, lightweight PETG (polyethylene terephtalate glyco) plastic material.

Using a folded plastic sheet that is extremely thin (0.75mm), these incredible geodesic structures are rigid and self-supporting. The beauty of this design lies in the use of such a thin sheet on such a large scale without the need for an internal framework to support it. Using the principle of origami, which uses the inherent strength of a fold to make three-dimensional structures, the design explores the application of a plastic in a new context. Another aspect that makes this project unique is that it eliminates the need to include fragile sheets of glass in order to obtain total transparency in a building.

The image shows the domes made from Spectar®, a transparent copolyester sheet from Eastman Chemicals. This material has massive potential in display and advertising due to its ability to deal with graffiti, as scratches and scuff marks can be removed with a heat gun.

Salute multipurpose wall cabinet
Designer: Harry Allen

The furniture and accessory manufacturer Magis has built a family of products that celebrates plastics in the home. Along the way, it has created some iconic designs in unexplored typologies, generating "happy and colorful projects that communicate exemplary design."

In this Magis project, Zylar®, a high-performance styrenic, has been used in a product that requires a particular toughness. Zylar® is an impact-modified SAN (styrene acrylonitrile), formulated as a stiff, resilient, easy-to-process, and competitively priced alternative to other terpolymers, such as ABS (acrylonitrile butadiene styrene). According to the producers, Nova Chemicals, Zylar® is also more cost-effective during molding than traditionally tough polycarbonate.

Dimensions	**550x550mm**
Features	**Water-clear; Tough**
	Colors and decorates easily
	Easy to process
	Chemical and alcohol resistant
	FDA and USP Class VI-compliant
	Antistatic and indoor UV grades available
More	**www.novachemicals.com**
	www.zylar.com/main.htm
	www.magisdesign.it
Applications	**Toys, computer accessories, cosmetics packaging, medical devices, water filter jugs, point of sale, tap handles, office work tools, house wares.**

Celebrating plastic

Dense and light

The wonderful quality that EPP (expanded polypropylene) has to offer is that it combines an incredibly lightweight structure with outstanding density relative to its weight.

EPP can be formed into large solid-wall thicknesses. It can also be colored or printed, and surface patterns and graphics can be molded into the surface. Chairs can also be made available with different color combinations in the same components, giving a mottled, multicolored effect.

Apart from standalone components and products, various manufacturers have also developed technology where EPP can be molded directly into the casings of other components, thereby reducing assembly times and costs.

If you look at this material without any preconceptions of its more typical applications, it frees your mind to a world of new possibilities for this underused material and its unique set of characteristics.

Features	**Excellent energy absorption**
	Very good cushioning
	High service temperature
	Available in a range of densities
	Colorable; Recyclable
More	**www.styreneforum.org**
	www.tuscarora.com
Applications	**Surfboards, bicycle helmets, fruit and vegetable trays, insulation blocks, head-impact protection in car headrests, bumper cores, steering column fillers, acoustic dampening.**

Sample of EPP foam used as a flexible cushion

It is always interesting to see material combinations. In composites, the physical and visual properties work off each other to create new technologies with enhanced properties. Interesting effects can also be created from "marriages" of materials.

These containers from Alessi combine two materials: corrosion- and scratch-resistant stainless steel, and a transparent acrylic peripheral skin. This combination links the production and material heritage of Alessi's stainless steel collections with a move to plastics.

Acrylic was used for aircraft cockpit covers in WWII, a time when the transparency of plastic was expected to take over from glass in the automotive industry. Today, acrylic is still the choice for clarity and is often viewed as the material closest to glass in this respect.

Unless blended with other plastics such as PVC, which improves its impact strength, acrylic does have some of the fragility of glass. There are other materials, such as polystyrene, PET, SAN, and polycarbonate that compete for clarity, but acrylic falls between polystyrene and polycarbonate for cost.

Apart from its availability as a resin, it is also a hugely popular sheet material sold under the Perspex, Plexiglas, or Lucite trade names.

Dimensions	**Small Love bowls 120x50mm**
	Super Love bowl 300x100mm
Features	**Sparkling clarity**
	Good hardness and stiffness
	Good weatherability
	Good chemical resistance
	Available in a range of semi-finished rods, tubes, and sheets
More	**www.alessi.com**
	www.ineosacrylic.com
Applications	**Paints, fabrics, domestic appliances, lighting, furniture, glazing, interior screens, lenses, signage, car tail lights, furniture. Acrylic is also the main ingredient for DuPont's solid surface material Corian®.**

Glass-like clarity

Love bowls
Designer: Miriam Mirri
Manufacturer: Alessi

212 On Ice perfume bottle
Designer: Carolina Herrera NY
Manufacturer: Antonio Puig, S.A.

Features	**Tough**
	Colors and decorates easily by print, hot stamp, and metalizing
	Sparkling clarity
	Lower density means more parts per kilogram of resin
	Low-cost processing
	Chemical resistant
	Alcohol resistant
	UL94 HB-approved
	FDA and USP Class VI-compliant
	Antistatic and indoor UV grades available
More	**www.novachem.com**
Applications	**Tumblers, perfume bottle caps, handles for taps, medical devices, toys, waterfilter jugs, domestic cleaning appliances, transparent rigid coat hangers.**

Clear alternative

There is a seductiveness about a material that is solid and tough enough to withstand abuse but which has a water-like clarity. Clarity has been a preoccupation of design since the first clear plastics were developed. The molding of clarity offers our senses the chance to be cheated with solid, rigid enclosures containing electronics, packaging, and other objects.

Nas® is a brand of SMMA (styrene methylmethacrylate copolymer) from Nova Chemicals. It is marketed as a transparent alternative to SAN, clear polystyrene, and acrylic, or for applications that require strong, stiff, clear components. It is also promoted as a lower-cost alternative to some of these plastics due to its ease of processing and lower density, which means more parts per kilogram of resin.

We take it for granted that transparent plastics are unexceptional, but before the invention of this relatively new material the only thing that was transparent was glass. Constricted by its fragility, risk when broken, and molding limitations, glass's impact on mass-production has been limited. The introduction of clear plastics heralded a quiet revolution in packaging, furniture, safety devices, medical, transport, and a wealth of other markets.

Can-do colors

The transparency of plastics has been one of the key reasons for their use in replacing traditional materials.

ABS is a terpolymer made up from three components, or, in technical terms, three monomers. A typical blend of ABS contains about 20 percent rubber, 25 percent acrylonitrile, and 55 percent styrene. It is a material that is primarily categorized by its toughness, but is also notable for its ease of processing, low cost, and transparency.

The introduction of transparency into the molding of plastics has allowed designers to create objects that would previously have required an exceptional level of craftsmanship, or which would have been impossible.

Karim Rashid has ventured into nearly every area of design, including furniture, textiles, and even pet products. Following on from the success of his Garbino trashcan, Rashid has produced a series of new cans. These reflect the linear, veined, optical qualities of automobile tail lights and display an honest approach to waste, allowing a colored vapor to surround the visible contents and contribute to the domestic landscape.

Dimensions	**260x305mm**
Features	**High-impact strength, even at low temperatures**
	Low cost
	Versatile production
	Good resistance to chemicals
	Good dimensional stability
	Hard and scratch resistant
	Flame resistant
	Can achieve a high gloss
	Excellent mechanical strength and stiffness
More	**www.karimrashid.com**
	www.geplastics.com
	www.basf.com
Applications	**White goods, telephones, housings for consumer electronics, vacuum cleaners, car parts, food processors, cellphone casings.**

Afterglow Can
Design: Karim Rashid
Client: Umbra

Plastic to go

Features	**Quite brittle in its pure form; blending it increases strength but reduces optical clarity**
	Food safe
	Easy to mold
	Clear and low cost
	Low shrinkage rate
	Low moisture absorption
More	**www.dow.com/styron/index.htm**
	www.huntsman.com
	www.atofina.com
Applications	**Disposable cutlery, pens, and razors; cups; plates; food packaging; packing materials; thermal insulation; CD cases; refrigerator compartments; model kits.**

Disposable coffee-cup lids are a product of our time; they are a cultural statement about our habits, fashions, and lifestyles. It seems that for every cup of coffee there is a different product, with its own strangely decorated channels, from the lid that you completely remove to the lid with tearable flaps or sliding doors.

Within these peculiarly decorated functional surfaces is an interface between the drink and our lips. This landscape of ribs, channels, and text gives us clues about the material and molding technologies. These are structural forms that owe their shape to a combination of mechanics and aesthetics.

With regards to the material, polystyrene is from the commodity group of plastics—materials that are common, easy to mold, and cheap. On its own, polystyrene is quite a brittle material, but, as with many other commodity plastics, it crosses boundaries between resins, foams, and grades of impact resistance.

Power stools

Miura Bar Stool

This stool is a wonderful combination of material and product. Within its dynamic, stealth aesthetic lays an example of a structural use of plastic that is rarely seen.

There are chairs and stools that combine stable shapes and thin wall thickness to create strong structures, but they all seem to follow the same principles of form combined with established material.

What Miura offers us through this shape is almost unprecedented as a plastic molding in a single piece, with its off-balance structure and cantilevered seat looking instead like something that should be cast from aluminum. Indeed, the manufacturers of this stool claim it is two-and-a-half times stronger than aluminum.

In its pure state polypropylene can be easily tailored to control its various features. For a commodity plastic it is reasonably stiff and rigid but, as with any plastic, the addition of reinforcement takes it to new levels of strength and stiffness.

Dimensions	**470x400x810mm**
Features	**Widely available**
	Low density
	Good strength and rigidity
	Cost-effective
	Ability to incorporate live hinges
	Good chemical resistance
	Recyclable
More	**www.plank.it**
	www.konstantin-grcic.com
Applications	**Food and nonfood packaging, centrifugal tubes and disposable syringes for the medical industry, blow-molded bottles, food containers.**

Plastic as brand

Dimensions	250x105x330mm
Features	**Waxy; Easy to mold**
	Tough at low temperatures
	Low cost; Flexible
	Good chemical resistance
More	**www.karimrashid.com**
	www.methodhome.com
Applications	**Chemical drums, toys, kitchenware, cable insulation, carrier bags, car fuel tanks, furniture, Tupperware.**

Plastic has slowly replaced many other materials in packaging applications. Ever since rust-resistant polypropylene was used to replace heavy, awkward, steel paint tins, plastics have proved user-friendly alternatives to metals, glass, and other materials.

The squeezy, succulent, and curvy outline of this soap bottle not only makes for a logical ergonomic shape, but also a highly distinctive brand identity. Designer Karim Rashid has created a language of shape and color that is individual while also appealing to the mass market. There is no difference in the basic material from any ordinary soap bottle, but the use of translucent material, sensuous curves, and silky, waxy surface (combined with the smell of the soap) provide a multisensory experience.

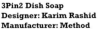

3Pin2 Dish Soap
Designer: Karim Rashid
Manufacturer: Method

m

method

dish soap
concentrated formula
aroma: mint

25 fl oz (739ml)

How to use:
- Pour very hot water, approximately 194°F (90°C), into a bowl or pan
- Immerse the handle in the water for approximately five minutes until soft
- Remove from water with tongs or other safe equipment
- While still soft but cool enough to hold, form the handle into the desired shape to fit the user's needs
- When satisfied with the shape, place handle into cold water to harden. The metal head part is pushed into the handle while the latter is soft (no bonding agent is used). Therefore it is possible to turn the head part into a desired position to fit the user's needs while the handle is still soft

Warning:
- Head part becomes very hot when it is placed in hot water. Be sure to use protective gloves
- Do not place reshaped handle in cold water while it is still on the user's hand or it may never be removed from their hand after cooling and hardening
- Do not expose to direct flame. Material is inflammable and will melt at a high temperature

114

Roll with it

The most common way of classifying plastics is thermoset and thermoplastics groupings. However, within these groupings there are other ways of classifying materials in order to make selecting the right application easier.

Polyolefins exist in the thermoplastics branch, alongside vinyls and styrenes. Polyolefins, however, account for the largest volume of all resins in world production, with about one-third accounted for by polyethylene. Polyethylene is a major part of this group, partly due to its availability in different densities. The most common types of PE are low, medium, and high. It is also available as ultra-high molecular weight.

Made from a blow-molding grade of high-density polyethylene, this chair by Ron Arad for Magis allows for a seamless form in this resilient material.

Dimensions	784x601x1,148mm
Features	Rigid; Low-impact strength
	High-tensile strength
	Waxy; Easy to mold
	Tough at low temperatures
	Low cost; Flexible
	Good chemical resistance
More	www.magisdesign.com
	www.ronarad.com
	www.cpchem.com
Applications	Toys, kitchenware, sporting goods, carrier bags, furniture.

Voido chair
Designer: Ron Arad
Client: Magis

The most banal applications of materials can disguise the fact that they have far richer applications than we might assume. Fitting snugly between the walls of the cardboard box and the protected product inside it is a humble, low-density, solid material that has unexplored potential: expanded polystyrene (EPS).

The production of polystyrene foam is based on tiny polystyrene beads that are expanded to 40 times their original size using a flow of steam and pentane. Steam is also used in the final phase to inject the material into the mold. In comparison to EPP foam, polystyrene is less of a performance material, not having the range of densities, flexibility, and strength.

Although it is 98 percent air, polystyrene is often perceived as not being a friend of the environment. However, industry is keen to point out that polystyrene foam has never used CFCs (chlorofluorocarbons) or HCFCs (hydrochlorofluorocarbons) during production. Perception of the big and bulky bits of packaging not being recycled but left to accumulate also enforces this perception. As a result, major steps have been taken to provide recycling facilities. Once collected, the waste can be compacted and used to remold in its compacted form or ground down to form new products.

98 percent air

Dimensions	1,050x1,875x400mm	Cloud Modules Designers: Ronan & Erwan Bouroullec
Features	Cheap; Lightweight; Durable	
	Good insulation properties	
	Shock absorbant; Insulating	
	Low hardness; Recyclable	
	Easily branded	
More	www.eps.co.uk	
	www.tuscarora.com	
	www.kay-metzeler.com	
	www.cappellini.it	
	www.bouroullec.com	
Applications	Disposable drinking cups for hot and cold drinks. Expanded polystyrene has also been used on a much larger scale; for example, in housing in the Netherlands as a buoyant platform. In horticultural applications, it is used to control temperature around root growth. Polystyrene foam is extruded and then thermoformed into trays and egg boxes.	

117 Smart Plastics

118

Plastic with a shelf life

Here's the idea. You are a busy person, with too many little jobs that fill your day: telephone calls, appointments, etc. You want to rent a movie, but first you have to drive to the store to pick it up and again later, to return the disc. Time taking your DVD back is wasted time. Can you really be bothered?

But then you find out about Flexplay, a type of DVD that expires 48 hours after opening the package. No need to take the movie back; just let the information die. Unopened, the disc stays "fresh" in the package for about a year. Once exposed to oxygen, you have 48 hours to play the disc as many times as you want in any standard DVD player. After 48 hours, your time is up and the disc turns from bright red to black and is no longer playable. Just recycle the now-useless polycarbonate disc.

What is most interesting about this technology is that it raises the question: what if more products and plastics were like organic matter, and had shorter natural lifespans?

Dimensions	**120mm diameter**
Features	**Data with a shelf life**
More	**www.flexplay.com**
	www.geplastics.com

Flexplay ez-D™
48-hour no-return DVD
Manufacturer: Flexplay
Technologies, Inc

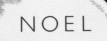

Industrial component made by nanomolding aluminum to plastic

The impact of nanotechnology has yet to be felt in consumer applications. It is, however, an area of materials research that guarantees to provide a massive change in how materials can be used and what they will, ultimately, be able to do. This case study uses a form of nanotechnology in the bonding of materials.

Injection assembly technology was developed to allow for different plastic materials to be bonded with aluminum in the injection-molding tool during the molding process. The process is based in the use of a nanotechnology to indent the surface of the aluminum so that it acts like an anchor for the plastic resin. The nano surface is applied by dipping the aluminum in a liquid solution, where the surface is transformed from a plate-like structure into an almost porous arrangement. The metal blank is then inserted into the mold, onto which the resin is injected. The resulting bond is extremely strong, forming a joint that is as strong as the material itself. Apart from allowing cost reductions through reduced assembly times, it also allows for functions and material combinations that otherwise might have been problematic.

Nanoanchors

Features	Nonbreakable
	Permanent bond
	Lightweight
	Cost-effective at integrating metal and plastic resin
	Large choice of elastomer hardnesses
More	www.taiseiplas.com/e
Applications	PDAs and computers, bicycles, automotive applications, large-scale components for architecture. The technology can also offer a soft texture, which is useful for impact absorption and nonslip surfaces.

120

Handformed plastic

This is a material that you can indulge your senses in. It is a material that thinks it's a lump of plasticine. It can go from hot, soft, and sweaty to a cold and machineable hardness, and then back again. Polymorph is a plastic that is more at home in a classroom than a factory.

Polymorph is a polyethylene-based plastic that, in its method of forming, exhibits the potential to be closer to a lump of clay than to granules for injection molding. The principle behind it is the fact that all plastics soften and become malleable when heated. What makes this material so special, however, is that it becomes malleable at a relatively low temperature, which makes it accessible on a low-tech scale.

The instructions ask that you place the granules inside a bowl of hot water or heat them with a hairdryer until they soften and join together to form a solid mass. Once it has reached this state, you can play with the soft but still stiff dough to your heart's content or until it cools down and starts to harden. Once this happens, you can machine it or cut it like any other plastic. When you are tired of that, you just heat it up and make something else. It brings plastic to a completely new venue; a place where it can be formed by hand in a manner that is closer to cooking than anything formed by mass production.

Features	**Easily formed without tooling**
	Cost-effective
	Easily available
	Can be melted and reused
More	**www.maplin.co.uk**
Applications	**The basic principle of allowing a plastic to be handformed means that it can be used for making prototypes, formers for vacuum-forming, and molds for casting.**

Shape-memory resins offer an invitation to push the limits of new technologies into new product areas and new functions for products. In their simplest form they are like toys, waiting for the playful experimentation that will lead to new product applications.

CRG Industries has developed a range of products based on the shape-memory effect. Veriflex™ is an advanced two-part memory resin. The effect occurs when the plastic is heated above its activation point, where it changes from being stiff and inflexible to a limp, elastic state, when it can be bent, twisted, pulled, and stretched up to 200 percent. When cooled, the plastic returns to its hardened form. It retains this shape indefinitely or until heated again past its activation point, when it returns to its original form. This process can be repeated indefinitely. The beauty of this technology is that it allows for products to be molded using conventional techniques such as injection molding.

With the addition of a thermochromic pigment, the resin can have extra functionality, allowing for a change of color when it has reached its activation point. This eliminates the problems of overheating the material.

Memories are made of this

Features	**Can return to a programmed memory shape**
	Can be repeatedly heated and reformed
	High stiffness
	Transportable as flat sheet
	High strength at low temperatures
More	**www.crg-industries.com**
Applications	**Customizable and reusable molds, architecture, furniture, deployment mechanisms, containers, shipping/ packaging, toys, actuators.**

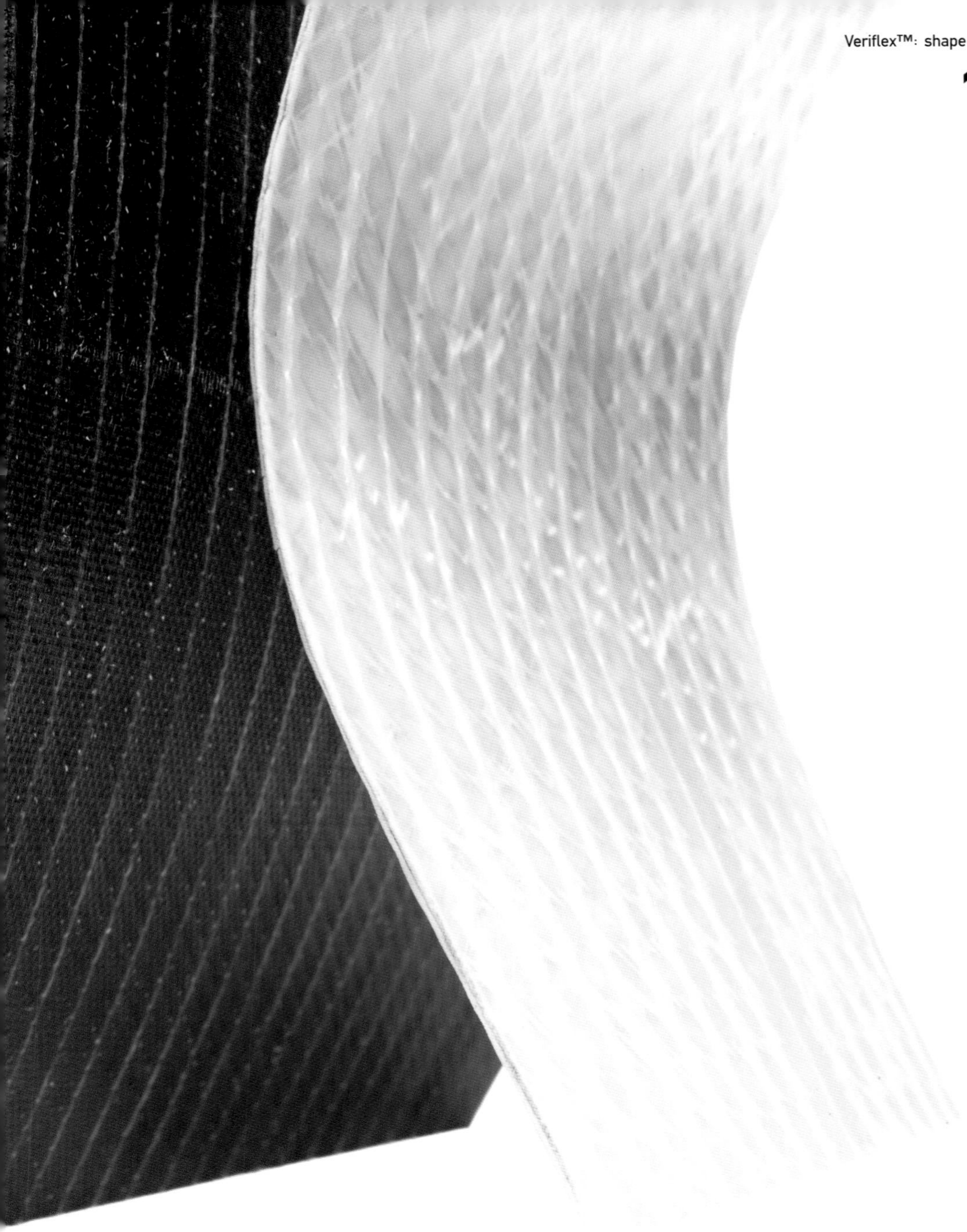

The world of shape-memory materials is
a rich and fascinating one that includes
metals, plastics, fabrics, sheet materials,
and now foams. Unlike the metal and
plastic varieties, this foam does not use
heat to return to a "remembered" profile.
Instead, the material displays a much
more modest effect, similar to a super-
viscous liquid that allows for a slow
release of an imprint that has been
pushed into its surface.

This range of high-memory or shock-
absorbing foams (SAFs) is available in
several grades of softness and elasticity.
As with viscoelastic foams, they react to
gradual force with a viscous behavior,
and absorb shock-like forces with elastic
behavior. This behavior depends on
temperature, as the material becomes
more pliable when it is warm. This
makes it good for mattresses, for
example, as body warmth makes it
more adaptable.

Shock-absorbing foam is used in
orthopedic and medical mattresses and
cushions to prevent bedsores. It offers
support similar to gel or liquid cushions.
The open-cell, porous structure also
allows the material to breathe.

Features	Good impact absorption
	Has a small degree of memory
	Even distribution of pressure
More	www.foampartner.com
Applications	Orthopedic bed mattresses, cushions, and shoes; sound absorption and dampening; impact absorption. Has also been used in flooring.

Shock-absorbing foam

Supergels

EdiZONE LC invents new technologies and develops them into products that are licensed to various markets. They have developed a core of three basic technologies in the area of what can be described as supergels and foams. Within this range of technologies lies three fantastically soft gel-cushioning materials: Gelastic™, Intelli-Gel™, and Floam™.

Gelastic™ is a thermoplastic elastomeric copolymer gel, so it can be extruded, cast, or injection molded. It can be formulated into a range of hardnesses and is extremely strong.

Gelastic™ forms the basis for a second technology: Intelli-Gel™. This is a semiformed material that combines the intrinsic cushioning qualities of Gelastic™ into a cell structure. This exploits the effect of column buckling to allow objects to sink into the cushion without increasing the unit pressure of the object.

Floam™, or Z-Flo™ as it is known in some markets, is the world's lightest nongas fluid. It is used as a filling inside a plastic bladder to distribute pressure evenly in applications such as hospital bedding to prevent bedsores.

Although generally used under a secondary skin and not exposed, these plastics are some of the most seductive materials you will find. They have a beautiful tinted translucency and the feel of a slightly sticky, semiwet sponge.

Behind this rich range of sensuous playfulness lies a selection of materials with serious applications. However, EdiZONE is keen to point out that no matter how exciting the potential for the materials appears, they are strictly for high-volume mass production.

Features	**Very stable**
	Close to body temperature
	Does not alter properties with changes in temperature
	Superstrong
More	**www.edizone.com**
Applications	**These materials are used in a wide range of cushioning products. The principle behind the materials is that they distribute pressure over the whole object that it is cushioned. Thus applications include surgical tourniquets, which are used to prevent damage to tissue while preventing excessive bleeding during surgery. Nike has used Floam™ under the name Nike Form in football and baseball cleats, snowboard boots, and skates. Other applications for Floam™ include orthopedic support products and hospital bed mattresses for long-term care. Intelli-Gel™ is used as cushioning for the body, vibration dampening, and impact absorption. Finally, probably the most fun application is for a child's ultra-light, bouncy toy that uses the material as a molding compound.**

**Sample of Intelli-Gel™
Manufacturer:
Edizone LC**

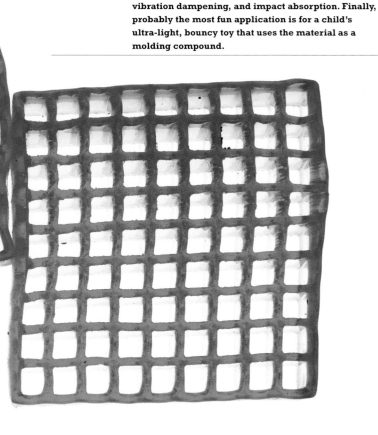

HydroSpan™

128

**Sample of semi-swelled
HydroSpan™
Manufacturer:
Industrial Polymers**

Grow your own

Grow your own products with this flexible urethane resin! HydroSpan™ is a polyurethane-based product developed by Industrial Polymers. It relies on mixing together three main ingredients: hardener, resin, and plain water. As you would expect, the addition of water makes this stuff grow.

The process involves mixing the resin and hardener to make your component, which can be formed in a mold. In order to enlarge the cured part, it is left in a bath of water. The length of time required for the part to soak depends on its size and thickness. The manufacturers recommend that a part with a one-inch wall thickness will require about 14 days to expand to a maximum of 60 percent. The product can be removed from the water at any time, depending on how much you want the piece to expand by. Once the part is fully soaked, the water is trapped inside the polymer matrix and the part feels completely dry. After several months, the material returns to its original size unless kept immersed in water. In terms of hardness, it feels like a stiff jelly, with a hardness of 45 Shore in its nonexpanded state, and a slightly softer 35 Shore in its expanded state.

Features	Ability to expand
	Relatively cheap
	Can be used without any big tooling on a craft scale
More	www.industrialpolymers.com
Applications	This material is described by Industrial Polymers as being like a "three-dimensional copy machine" and is promoted as a modeling material. Other applications could include toys or applications that use the reverse effect, exploiting the ability of the material to shrink when the water content dries out.

131 Engineering Polymers

132

Silicone enhancements

Magic Trivet
Designers: Jackie Piper
& Victoria Whitbread
Manufacturer: W2

For a moment, let's ignore the fact that silicone is a high-performance, high-cost material, and instead talk about its sensuous assets as one of the most pleasurable and playful plastics. W2 has built a collection of silicone-based products that takes common domestic bathware, tableware, and kitchenware, and reinterprets these into cheerful, design-led forms, shapes, and textures with a close relationship to the actual functions of the products. Part of the massive attraction of these items is their soft, colored translucency, which appeals on a variety of sensuous levels.

Utilizing the soft, gel-like quality of silicone, the W2 products exploit specific aspects of the material. The Magic Trivet utilizes the supreme heat-resistance of silicone combined with a thermochromic additive to produce a product that changes color according to the heat of the dish. The kitchen suckers use the suppleness of the material, while the candle holders exploit silicone's heat-resistance. All the products are celebrations of a bouncy and sometimes floppy material combined with forms that make standard everyday household accessories just a little more fun.

Dimensions	**230x330mm**
Features	**Floppy and bouncy**
	Heat and flame resistant
	Easy to color
	UV-resistant
	Food-safe
	Chemically inert
More	**www.w2products.com**
	www.primasil.com
	www.gesilicones.com
Applications	**Keypad elbow rests, oven door seals, breast implants, baking trays, surgical equipment, high temperature sealants, baby teats, silly putty.**

Mirror, mirror

Philips 639 cellphone
Designer: Philips
Design Team
Manufacturer: Philips

The idea behind this cellphone-cum-vanity-mirror is that, when closed, the front face is a mirror for checking personal grooming, but when incoming calls are received the caller ID is displayed through the mirror. The "Magic Mirror" technology that lies behind this is an electrically conductive polymer, an area of material research that is becoming ever more important.

Electrically conductive polymers were first discovered by accident in the 1970s. The story is that a student at the Tokyo Institute of Technology added too much catalyst to a batch of polyacetylene. The resulting silvery film was doped with various oxidizing agents and became conductive.

Today we are just at the beginning of the full impact that this technology will have on our lives. The continuing growth in display technologies is being pushed not only by research, but also by the consumer expectation that information should become available on an increasingly mobile and miniature scale. This pushes business to explore lighter, more reliable, and thinner display systems. The number of acronyms in this field is confusing, including OLEDs, LEPs, PLEDs, and PolyLEDs. All of these technologies are based on the same concept of organic electroluminescence.

Dimensions	**79x43x21mm**
Features	**Requires no backlight and therefore intrinsically thin**
	Lightweight; Bright; Clear
	Unlimited viewing angle
	High contrast
	Fast image refresh rate even at low temperatures
	Energy efficient
More	**www.research.philips.com**
	www.cdtltd.co.uk
Applications	**Flexible and formable displays, cellphones, PDAs, computers, and televisions. Large single-pixel displays can be used in lighting applications, replacing incandescent and fluorescent bulbs. New applications include advertising and signage, car dashboards, and instrument panels.**

Multitalented

Features	**Cost-effective**
	Easy to mold and color
	High abrasion resistance
	Resistant to oils and solvents
	High tear resistance
	Good resistance to weathering
	High flex life
	Low coefficient of friction
	Easy to machine
	Good impact strength
More	**www.wattsurethane.com**
	www.polyurethane.org
	www.cue-inc.com
	www.bayermaterialsciencenafta.com
Applications	**Polyurethanes are a highly prolific material found in many industrial and consumer applications, from wearable to heavy industry. In its cast form, applications include seals, belts, bumpers, cutting surfaces, and rollers. In consumer applications, it is used for soles of running shoes and shoe heels, fabric coatings, furniture, and as the ingredient for spandex and Lycra. It is also readily available as a molding compound and semiformed sheet, rod, and tube.**

Samples of a range
of off-the-shelf
polyurethane profiles
from Watts Urethanes

It is difficult to characterize some materials because they have the potential to exist in so many guises. Polyurethanes are one of these materials, existing in forms that range from foams to liquid coatings, and from rigid super-tough moldings to floppy gels and cast, droopy, rubbery sheets.

Urethanes are one of the five major groups of polymer classifications. The others are ethylenes, styrenes, vinyl chlorides, and esters. Part of the reason they can be converted into so many different forms is that, like PVC, urethanes can be produced as thermosets, thermoplastics, and rubbery forms. One of the largest areas for polyurethanes is in the production of foams, where they exhibit soft, spongy qualities. In their solid-cast form, they are playful, leathery, and sometimes elastic or rubber-like materials, which can easily be colored and have the toughness of metals.

In terms of abrasion resistance, they can be compared with nylon and acetyls, and so are an effective replacement for rubber, metal, and other plastics in abrasion-resistant applications. In terms of flexibility and general rubberiness, they are similar to TPUs, but without the adaptability of a range of molding techniques.

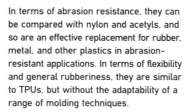

Features	**Combines the moldability of plastics with the flexibility of rubber**
	Highly resistant to flex fatigue, chemicals, abrasion, and tearing
	Interior and exterior use
	Hytrel® can be blow, injection and rotational molded, and extruded
	Breathable
More	**www.hermanmiller.com**
	www.quantum5280.com
	plastics.dupont.com
Applications	**Injection-molded bed springs, office furniture, and the breathable layers on antiallergenic bedding.**

Design is having to become increasingly interdisciplinary, looking beyond conventional approaches to material conventions within traditional typologies. Hytrel® is a material that lends itself to such an approach. Not restricted to being just a molding compound, it can also be tailored to create fabrics and yarns. From DuPont, Hytrel® fibers have been licensed to textile company Quantum Group Inc. for use in a range of upholstery applications.

One of the most high-profile products to feature the fabric is the Aeron chair, manufactured by Herman Miller. This has become a modern-day icon for office chair design. Using a stack of engineering plastics, including Hytrel®, it is a case study for how engineering plastics can be used for a host of structural applications.

New cushioning

As part of the brief to encompass pioneering ergonomics, the chair is designed to fit around the infinite range of human shapes and postures, taking into account the range of activities that take place during the day. The open-celled, breathable Hytrel® fabric that is used for the back and seat upholstery offers the design a sag-free, cushionable surface that replaces traditional foam.

**Aeron chair
Designers: Bill Stumpf and
Don Chadwick
Manufacturer: Herman Miller**

Features	**Weatherable; Colorfast**
	Impact and chemical resistant
	Resistant to environmental stress cracking
	Easy to process
	High heat resistance
	High gloss
More	**www.plasticsportal.com**
Applications	**Applications can be divided into three main markets: automotive, building/construction, and leisure. Specific products include garden furniture, sprinklers, garden lights, extruded glazing, and satellite aerials. Other applications include microwave ovens, vacuum cleaners, and washing machines.**

Welcome to the world of terpolymers: a place where the best bits of three monomers are blended to form a completely new material with a stack of new potential uses. One of the most prevalent terpolymers is ABS, a material known for its toughness and ease of production. Compared with ABS, ASA is probably less recognized but also has many uses.

ASAs can be summarized as a tough, robust, and durable material. Based on acrylonitrile, styrene, and acrylate, ASA resins have properties similar to ABS but with a rubber taking the place of the butadiene that exists in ABS. This rubber adds resilience to UV and oxygen degradation, which marks the main distinction and makes it a valuable material for outdoor use. It is this resistance to chemicals and impact, and its ability to hold colors, which mean that ASAs should be a main consideration for external, weatherable applications.

The outsider

**Oral-B CrossAction® Power electric toothbrush
Manufacturer: Braun**

Parton Swiss Army Knife
Designer: Victorinox
Manufacturer: Victorinox

In the 1930s, nylon (or polyamide, by its technical name) was one of the first engineering polymers to be discovered. Developed by DuPont, the nylon name has now become part of common language. Although existing in many forms, the properties across the family of resins vary due to the number of different formulations. However, nylon is characterized by strength, toughness, and stiffness.

Strength, toughness, and stiffness

The Swiss Army Knife provides the perfect symbol for this tough plastic, and is perhaps the perfect match of product with material. Both product and material are icons and are known for their ruggedness, with different versions and slight modifications and additions available. Two of the most widely used versions of nylon are nylon 6 and nylon 66. As a molding compound, it exhibits several superior qualities. When reinforced with glass, nylon becomes an even harder material. By itself, it is not one of the strongest engineering plastics, but has a natural waxy surface and the added advantage of being able to be cast.

Dimensions	**91x10mm**
Features	**Slippery**
	Good impact resistance
	Tough; Stiff
	Wear resistant
	Able to achieve a high gloss
	Available clear or opaque
More	**www.emsgrivory.com**
Applications	**Well known for being able to be drawn into silk-like fibers for clothing, nylon has a variety of uses and forms, including glass-reinforced molding compounds. Other applications include rope, engineering applications, and nutcrackers. Nylon is useful under the hood of cars, where its performance characteristics make it suitable for a variety of components. Low friction makes it useful for bearings, cams, and gears.**

Surgical precision

Features	High temperature resistance
	Chemical resistant
	High impact strength
	Tough; Rigid
	Transparent
	Biologically inert
	Easily processed
	Approved for food contact and potable water use
More	www.solvayadvancedpolymers.com
	www.solvayplastics.com
Applications	A large number of applications are in the medical industry, such as instrument trays, surgical equipment handles, and components that require products to be continually sterilized and to withstand being thrown around. Other applications where products require sterilization and high wear include canteen trays, electrical/electronic components, wire insulation, and parts for aircraft interiors.

Stainless steels are a common material in the medical arena; their corrosion resistance and general high-wearability have been unsurpassed. They are, however, limited on many levels. Enter polyphenyl sulfone (PPSU) plastics: thermoplastics that are characterized by their transparency, rigidity, and ability to remain stable at high temperatures.

This range of materials can withstand temperatures of up to 405°F (207°C) while maintaining their strength. In the medical industry, which requires products to be repeatedly sterilized, PPSUs are engineered to withstand the sterilization process and highly aggressive cleaners. In their natural form, PPSUs are also stable and self-extinguishable, whereas other materials need modifiers to offer this quality. PPSU resins can be formed using standard plastic molding techniques, or they can be machined.

Sample plaques of PPSU supplied by Solvay Plastics

PEEK coffee maker: boiler-pin and steam faucet
Manufacturer: Victrex

Regarded as one the highest-performance polymers available, polyetheretherketone (PEEK) has a long list of assets that make it attractive for a range of demanding applications. Characterized by high stiffness, heat resistance, and strength, PEEK demonstrates its superior nature in applications to replace aluminum and other metals in the aerospace industry.

The distinguishing benefit of PEEK is that it is melt-processable, which means that it can be formed using conventional molding machinery. This is not always the case with other high-performing plastics. It is one of the purest and most stable of polymers, which means that it does not contain additives that may be released during heating in the molding process. It is also implantable for use as body-part replacements in the medical industry.

Features	**Easy to process**
	Tough; Stiff
	Scratch and fatigue resistant
	High-temperature resistance
	Chemical resistant
	Radiation resistant
	Can be processed by standard processing methods
More	**www.victrex.com**
	www.invibio.com
Applications	**There aren't many applications where you would actually see this material and be able to admire its properties. Its high cost means that applications tend to be limited to engineering, where it is used for bearings, bushings, as a coating, and for electrical connectors. PEEK is also a high-performance protective tubing and is available in glass- or carbon-filled grades.**

PEEK performance plastic

The contender

There are many materials that have applications and formulations that are so diverse it is impossible to categorize them in a straightforward way. Surlyn® is one of these. It is one of the big engineering polymer brands from DuPont. An Ionomer resin, Surlyn® has several high-performance characteristics that make it valuable in a range of applications. It appears in the translucent clarity of the thick, injection-molded walls of a perfume bottle, in squeezable, soft, extruded shampoo tubes, and even in the tough, resilient skin on golf balls.

A big marketing drive from plastic producers often results in the benefits of some plastics over other materials being more widely recognized, offering a rationalization of existing materials and components. For example, plastics such as polypropylene are now widely known to be able to integrate live hinges within their moldings while avoiding using secondary materials. On the other hand, take the case of glass, which, although it can be a super-cheap raw material, can't be formed or molded into complex shapes as easily as plastic.

How the many, diverse advantages of Surlyn®, which exist in a range of applications, are communicated to designers is a problem for the brand owners. It might be simplest to label it as a tough, crystal-clear material with a thousand uses waiting to be explored.

Dimensions	**Each unit is 100mm long**
Features	**Outstanding impact toughness**
	Abrasion and scuff resistant
	Chemical resistant
	Water-clear transparency and clarity
	High melt strength
More	**www.dupont.com/industrial-polymers/surlyn/index.html**
Applications	**Dog chews, perfume bottles, golf balls, hockey helmets, footwear, bodyboards, bowling pins, tool handles, glass coating, ski boots, laminating film, automotive fascias, bath and kitchen door handles.**

**Surlyn® Discovery Kit
designed to convey the
sensorial characteristics
of Surlyn®
Designer: DuPont**

Heavy betting

To really appreciate the value embedded in this material, you need to feel its weight in your hands. Visually, it looks like a typical plastic: a high-gloss surface on a complex molded shape. But here lies the deception, because, unlike a typical plastic, high-gravity plastics are as heavy as a piece of steel. To put its weight into relative terms, high-gravity plastics can have densities up to 15g/cc. This is quite impressive when compared with aluminum, which has a specific gravity of 2.7, or steel, at 7.6g/cc.

Traditionally, one of the key benefits to using plastics is their ability to be molded into complex shapes and to be relatively lightweight, so why would you use a material that is heavier than necessary? The answer lies in the unique potential to create a combination of moldability and weight: look at the list opposite for some typical applications.

HGPs get their weight from the addition of either mineral or metal fillers, depending on the amount of weight you want to create. As a guide, metal fillers give a darker range of colors than the naturally lighter minerals. As with high-performance engineering materials such as the more traditional, weighty, glass-filled nylon, HGPs are relatively expensive.

Features	**Heavy**
	Fillers can be combined with a range of plastics
	Can be used on standard molding equipment
More	**www.rtpcompany.com**
Applications	**Combining the ability to be processed like plastic with the perception of weight, high-gravity material is used for premium items such as perfume bottles and casino chips. Other consumer applications rely on the use of this material to add value to products by making them weighty. High-gravity compounds are used in fishing line weights, inserts for golf clubs to enhance balance, molded x-ray shields in the medical scanning industry, submersible components that need to be molded, sound dampening, and surgical instruments where balance and weight are important.**

Engineering your comfort

Hytrel® is one of the main engineering polymers from DuPont. TPEs (thermoplastic elastomers), as with many other plastics, can be formed into many varieties and forms. From its use as a fiber in industrial textiles, to a replacement metal that exploits its natural springiness, Hytrel® crops up in many unexpected places.

What is particularly interesting about this pillow by designers Maaike Evers and Mike Simonian is that they take the material out of the traditional context of engineering and into the arena of soft furnishings, challenging the possibilities of plastics in a domestic environment.

The pillows mark a new territory for this prolific material, exploiting its combination of the flexibility of rubbers with the strength and processability of plastic. It also integrates mold-in snap fittings and variable wall thickness, and can withstand repetitive bending. The reduction of mass and surface area also provides an efficient form. This not only results in a long-lasting, durable, and easy-to-clean product, but also provides a new visual language for a very traditional product typology.

**Thermoplastic Pillow Collection
Designers: Maaike Evers and
Mike Simonian**

Dimensions	350x350x80mm
Features	**Combines the moldability of plastics with the flexibility of rubber**
	Highly resistant to flex fatigue, chemicals, abrasion, and tearing
	Interior and exterior use
	Can be blow, injection, and rotational molded, or extruded
	Breathable
More	**www.mikeandmaaike.com**
	plastics.dupont.com

Applications

Hytrel® is a highly morphable material, lending itself to a range of forms that exploit its diverse properties. It has been used as an injection-molded bedspring, exploiting its strength and flexibility, and in a breathable layer on bedding such as antiallergenic mattresses, quilts, and pillow covers.

Beba children's night-light
Designer: Miriam Mirri
Manufacturer: Alessi

Inherent toughness

In metallurgists' terms, the words hardness, toughness, and strength have very specific meanings. Toughness is defined as the ability of a material to absorb energy by plastic deformation—an intermediate characteristic between softness and brittleness. The toughness of a product is characterized by impact strength and is only partly dependent on the material: other contributing factors include the way the component is molded, wall thicknesses, and part geometries. There are also factors such as the working temperature of the product and whether it is reinforced, as many materials can be made using various fibers.

However, there are materials that are tough due to their inherent strength. One of the most common and toughest engineering plastics is polycarbonate, which combines this toughness, stiffness, and strength with a superb optical clarity. Discovered in 1953, polycarbonate was originally used for electrical devices before being used for glazing.

In terms of clarity, polycarbonate can be compared with polystyrene, SAN, acrylic, and PET. For its toughness, it can be compared with acetals. One of the uses of polycarbonate resins is in blending with other plastics, such as ABS and PBT. The toughness of this widely used plastic is put to good use in the everyday application of this children's night-light.

Dimensions	**125x80x95mm**
Features	**Tough; Stiff; Strong**
	Water-like transparency
	Flame resistant
	Excellent dimensional stability, even at high temperatures
	Good heat resistance up to 257°F (125°C)
	Recyclable
	UV-stable; Nontoxic
More	**www.alessi.com**
Applications	**CDs and DVDs, visors and safety helmets, eyewear, kitchen containers, computer housings, architectural glazing, cellphone housings, packaging, automotive headlamps, shatter-resistant waterfountain bottles, riot shields, vandal-proof glazing. Polycarbonates are also used in the electrical and electronics industries.**

150

Metal replacement

Material families such as metals, ceramics, and plastics are always trying to find new markets in each other's industries: ceramics that can be molded like plastics; engineered woods that are as dense as aluminum; and now plastics that are trying to outperform metals. The advantage of plastics is quite evident: easy manufacturing in a virtually infinite range of shapes, colorability, and corrosion resistance. However, plastics traditionally fall short on the qualities of stiffness, strength, and hardness.

Parmax® addresses these shortfalls. It is a high-tech, high-performance engineering polymer that is part of the family of metal-replacement plastics engineered to outperform similar plastic rivals such as PEEK in strength. Unlike other superstrong plastics, Parmax® has no other reinforcing binders. Nonetheless, the manufacturers claim that Parmax® is two to three times stronger and stiffer than conventional unfilled thermoplastics.

The stiffness, strength, and hardness of Parmax® can be seen when you hold a sample in your hand: its high density and hardness more closely resemble a chunk of aluminum than plastic, although its shiny surface leaves no doubt that it definitely is a plastic.

Features	**High strength and stiffness**
	Excellent scratch resistance
	Good friction and wear properties
	Excellent chemical resistance
	Exceptional low-temperature performance
More	**www.mptpolymers.com**
Applications	**The low weight of Parmax® self-reinforced polymers makes them ideal as a metal replacement in weight-sensitive applications. Components can be compression-molded, extruded, cast, foamed, injection molded, and machined. This range of manufacturing potential makes it useful in a variety of commercial engineering applications, from films and coatings to aircraft interiors and surgical instruments.**

Nut and bolt made from Parmax
Manufacturer: MPT Polymers

Strong, lightweight, and soft

Aramid fiber is strong enough to moor the largest of Navy vessels and provide body protection against bullets, soft enough to use as gloves to protect against sharp metal and glass, and heat resistant enough to act as shielding in jet aircraft engines.

More commonly known as Kevlar®, like carbon and glass fiber it is available in various forms such as fabric and prepreg, thread, continuous filament yarn, and floc. This fiber, which for the same weight-to-weight ratio is five times stronger than steel, was developed in 1965 by DuPont. The shoe uses a sole plate made from Kevlar®, which provides improved sole stiffness, while at the same time absorbing impact forces, spreading the load over the whole area of the sole.

Features	**Low thermal shrinkage**
	Excellent dimensional stability
	High tensile strength at low weight
	Low elongation to break
	High cut resistance; High toughness
	High chemical resistance
	High modulus (structural rigidity)
	Low electrical conductivity
	Flame resistant
More	**www.dupont.com/kevlar/whatiskevlar.htm**
	www.hexcel.com
	www.dupont.com/kevlar/europe/
	www.e-composites.com/seal.htm
	www.saati.it/seal/ita/default.htm
Applications	**Adhesives and sealants, composites, body armor, bulletproof vests.**

Tough and flexible

Acetal is one of the stiffest and strongest polymers. Since its introduction in the 1960s its unique properties have bridged the gap between metals and other plastics within a huge range of applications from snap-fit clips, where it is used for its high spring resistance, to cigarette lighters, where it is used for chemical resistance. It's not flexible in the same way as certain elastomers or polypropylene but is much stiffer and generally not as pretty or as tactile.

Features	**High rigidity; Natural lubrication**
	High mechanical strength
	Excellent fatigue resistance
	Gloss finish
	High resistance to repeated impacts
	Toughness at low temperatures
	Excellent resistance to chemicals
	Excellent dimensional stability
	Good electrical insulating characteristics
	Good temperature range; Resilient
More	**www.dupont.com/enggpolymers/europe/**
	www.basf.com
Applications	**Fasteners, shower heads, hardware housings, snap fit buckles, clothes pegs, rollerblade brakes.**

**Delrin® clothes pegs
DuPont**

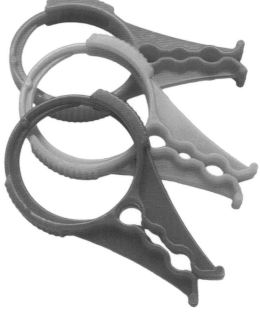

Imagine a material that feels like skin. It breathes and stretches, but can be cast or formed into any shape at any thickness. These properties were first applied in the medical and orthopaedic industry as cushioning for hospital patients. Technogel® is, however, one of those materials that through experimentation has branched into more popular domestic arenas.

Like skin

Technogel® is both a liquid and a solid at the same time. Products are produced by pouring the liquid into molds, which means it can be easily cast to include other things. RVS (Royal Vacuum System) is a patented system, which consists of vacuum-fusing different components into a single item, without the need for stitching or glueing. This system is applied by Royal Medica in the production of bed cushions where a thin urethane film is fixed to the Technogel®. Other potential covers include Lycra®, PVC, PU, leather, and textiles. In the sheet form shapes can easily be stamped out or cut. Its main advantage over similar water- or silicone-based gels is that it does not contain plasticizers. This means that it does not lose its basic properties over time. It's the only gel that doesn't break, harden, or age.

Features	**Good pressure distribution**
	Breathable (good water absorption and release)
	Good recovery capability
	Easy to combine with decorative materials
	High shock absorption
	Sheer force absorption
	Adjustable Shore hardness
	High elasticity; Colorfast
	Can be glued
	Nonirritating to the skin
	Can be injection molded
More	**www.royalmedica.com**
	www.selleroyal.com
Applications	**Bicycle saddles, orthopedic seats/ cushions, shoe insoles, office chairs, tennis racket handles.**

Technogel®
Client: Selle Royal

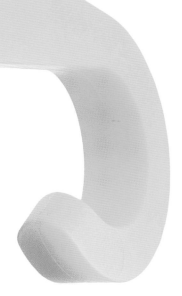

James doorstop
Client: Klein & More
Designer: Winfried Scheuer

Dishwasher safe

When Winfried Scheuer began designing the James doorstop, he was asked to create a soft object that would not damage the door. The use of the material TPE provided a good range of color possibilities compared with the more obvious choice of using rubber.

Because the product is injection molded in solid material the thickness at the thick end of the wedge needed to be controlled to stop sinkage marks forming. This happens when the inside plastic cools at a much slower rate than the outside surface. The dual function of the James was an outcome of a range of ideas that looked at the simple nontechnology of everyday household items that had previously been ignored. It comes in five colors and is dishwasher-safe. A fairly hard but still very flexible grade of TPE gives the James a very tactile quality.

Dimensions	**180x50mm**
Features	**Superior dynamic properties**
	Good cut and tear resistance at elevated temperatures
	Excellent oil, fuel, and solvent resistance
	Excellent flex fatigue resistance
	Soft and flexible material; High resilience
	Good range of processing techniques
	Excellent range of colors
More	**www.glscorporation.com**
	www.aestpe.com
Applications	**Hand grips, medical products, "O" rings, piping, offshore cabling, shock absorbers, sports shoes, side trims for cars, ski boots.**

Light Light
Designer: Takeshi
Ishiguro

The Light Light uses composites to create a featherly structure. Composites refer to a combination of two materials, a fiber-based material and a resin. In most modern composites the resins are usually made of polyester or epoxy. The fibers can be glass, carbon, aramid, polyethylene, or even natural fibers. The use of modern composites was pioneered by the aerospace industry when traditional materials did not provide high enough strength-to-weight ratio.

Prepregs are continuous sheets of fiber that are impregnated with resin. Fibers are arranged either in one direction, know as unidirectional (UD) or as a fabric with fibers arranged in several directions. They are typically used for high-tech automotive and aeronautical body panels and can be processed by tube rolling, pressure, or vacuum-bag processes and match molding. Fibers embedded into specific thermoset resins is the most widely used process. The areas of the product that require the greatest strength have thicker layers of fibers.

Hi-tech

Dimensions	**900x900mm**
Features	**Distinctive surface finish**
	Great strength-to-weight ratio
	Easy to customize; Range of shapes
	Available in a range of colors
	Good chemical resistance
	Noncorrosive; Extremely durable
	Neutral to aggressive environments
	Good temperature range
More	**www.globalcomposites.com**
	www.hexcel.com, www.carb.com
	www.composites.com
Applications	**Boats, automobiles, sports equipment, civil engineering, aeronautical parts, rail transport, architecture, toys.**

158

Tables of light

The idea of a flat sheet of plastic, which can reflect an even glow of light, has huge potential. The material is a light before you have even formed anything from it. It is a sheet of light waiting to be sculpted.

Prismex™ is the trade name given by Ineos for an acrylic panel which features a patented dot matrix screen-printed on to its surface. This allows the light to be reflected across the panel to produce a brilliant even illumination without the banding effect of conventional back-lit signs. Central to the design of both the Prismex™ Table and the Blow Prismex™ Pouffe is this lighting technology. Bobo Designs were the first to exploit the unique characteristics of Prismex™ acrylic sheet in the creation of contemporary furniture.

Dimensions	**1,800x1,000x720mm**
Features	**High energy efficiency; High melting point**
	Easy and versatile fabrication and processing
	Low-cost tooling
	Outstanding surface hardness and durability
	High print adhesion; Fully recyclable
More	**www.ineosacrylics.com, www.perspex.co.uk**
	www.bobodesign.co.uk, www.lucite.com
Applications	**Display, interiors, furniture, lighting, signage.**

Mutation of plastic and rubber

Features	**Exceptional toughness and resilience**
	High resistance to creep, impact, and flex fatigue
	High flexibility at low temperatures
	Maintains properties at high tempatures
	High resistance to industrial chemicals, oils, and solvents
	Good processing potential
	Good mechanical strength
	Excellent stretch and recovery characteristics
More	**www.dupont.com/enggpolymers/ products/hytrel**
	www.basf.com
Applications	**Springs, hinges, impact and sound absorbers, ski boots, textiles, furniture, engineering components, key pads.**

Hytrel® gives the flexibility of rubbers, the strength of plastics, and the processibility of thermoplastics. It is used in applications where mechanical strength and durability are required in a flexible component. Hytrel® is ideal for parts requiring excellent flex fatigue and ability to withstand a broad range of temperatures. It is highly resistant to tearing, flex-cut growth, creep, and abrasion.

Hytrel® is available in a full range of grades known as Shore D hardnesses. These range from a Shore D hardness of 72, which is quite rigid but still flexible, to a Shore D hardness of 35, which feels like a piece of rubber. Special grades include those that are heat stabilized, flame retardant, and blow molded. As with many polymers in their raw form the material comes in pellets, which are molded into the final products.

Bed Spring
Manufacturer: DuPont
Designer: Nike

Running Shoe
Designer: Nike

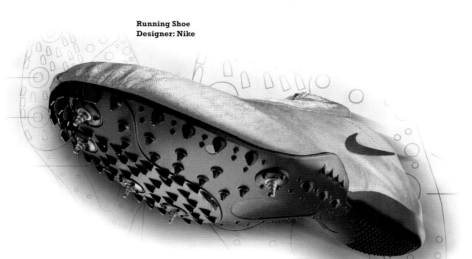

This shoe—designed for sprinter Michael Johnson—was made using Zytel®, a DuPont nylon polymer, and is a good illustration of a blend of materials coming together to fulfill a specific function. The main material is the nylon which is reinforced by 13 percent glass fiber to give it even more strength than it already has. This is combined with an elastomer to give the material flexibility without breaking.

Features	**High tensile strength**
	Excellent fatigue resistance
	Excellent flow properties
	Performance can be improved by fiber
	Withstands repeated impact
	Offers low coefficient of friction
	Fast molding cycles
	Resists abrasion and most chemicals
	Provides electrical insulation characteristics
More	**www.dupont.com/enggpolymers/ europe/news**
Applications	**Automotive, bearings, cams, gears, electrical appliances, industrial and consumer products.**

Featherly

Light thread

Features	Excellent abrasion resistance
	High tensile strength
	Excellent flow properties
	Excellent fatigue resistance
	Provides electrical insulation characteristics
	Withstands repeated impact
	Offers low coefficient of friction
	Fast molding cycles
	Resists abrasion and most chemicals
More	www.via.asso.fr
Applications	Tennis ball covers, upholstery, military apparel, abrasive pads, fishing line, parachutes, aircraft tire reinforcement, stockings, carpets.

The essence of this lighting design is its use of a forest of dyed nylon threads suspended in an inflatable structure, creating diffracted light. The piece is less about the design of a lighting form and more about the process of fabrication.

The nylon thread was provided by the textile manufacturer Tissavel, and is usually used in aerospace applications. The light is about a transfer of technologies where an industrial thread is used for a structural function within a domestic lighting application. The originality of the light comes from this unexpected utilization of a material and the soft light it gives.

Lamp
Designer: Francois
Azambourg

C360 Security Light
Designer: Mark Greene

Dimensions	**Thickness 3.5mm (including neoprene base)**
	Weight 7g (not including battery)
Features	**Uniquely thin displays**
	Versatile application; Good clarity of image
	Waterproof; Flexible
	Can be made transparent
	Excellent color range
More	**www.opsys.co.uk**
	www.uniax.com/165-0021.htm
Applications	**Armbands, vests, cycle helmets, cellphones, video phones and palm-top computers, furniture, ornamentation, advertising, smart cards, lighting.**

The use of polymers as light-emitting devices is not new, but a piece of plastic film less than 2mm thick which illuminates when attached to a battery still has a science-fiction "wow" factor to it and a huge as yet unfulfilled potential.

Using new bicycle frame geometry as a starting point, the product uses an existing material that offers 360° coverage of light, as opposed to conventional lights which are mono-directional. The wrap-around shape of a toilet-roll tube inspired the original pattern shape. The light is powered by a 9-volt battery which is connected by a drive unit to convert the power to a 110-volt AC current which is needed to light the film. The battery and drive unit are both housed under the seat. The film itself is mounted on to a thin sheet of neoprene, which acts as cushioning and grip for the film. The glow from this thin film provides enough light for the cyclist to be seen from a good distance, also giving 180–200 hours of continuous use.

No longer science fiction

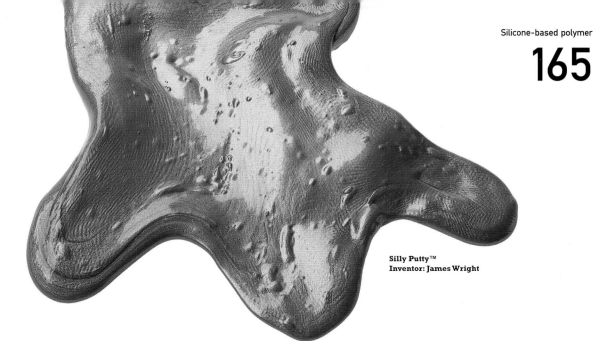

Silly Putty™
Inventor: James Wright

Bouncy stretchy

Features	
	Gradually flattens with gravity
	Bounces back 80% of the height from which it is dropped
	A dilatant compound, i.e. acts like a solid and retains its shape if pressure is applied quickly to it and behaves more like a liquid and is easily molded if pressure is applied slowly to it
	Cooling greatly improves its ability to bounce
	Shaped into a boat it will float on water
	Molded into a ball it will sink
	Nontoxic and nonirritating
	Highly elastic
More	**www.sillyputty.com**

In 1943, engineer James Wright, working for General Electric, was in his laboratory mixing substances in test tubes. He happened to combine boric acid and silicone oil and this compound became "polymerized." Wright extracted this gooey concoction from the test-tube and while doing so threw some on the floor. To his amazement, it bounced and so bouncing putty was born.

Determined to find a practical use for his creation, but to no avail, eventually Silly Putty was introduced at the International Toy Fair in New York in 1950. Silly Putty has since become a toy classic, quite literally a household name.

Attila can crusher
Client: Rexite Spa
Designer: Julian Brown

Avoiding the more expensive choice of material such as polycarbonate and acetal this product uses its own form and structure to fulfill this Herculean function. To enable 600 Newtons to crush an aluminum or steel can to 22mm in height it uses ABS in a series of intelligent webs and supports.

The original prototype was made in MDF as a test for the mechanism. Attila was then prototyped from a solid block of Delrin®, a very rigid material which proved the point that a polymer could stand up to the job. It proved in fact that the acetal was even too strong. This led to the choice of ABS as the material for the final product.

Attila addresses the environmental concerns of excessive consumption with one of the biggest symbols, the drinks can. It was important that in terms of materials and aesthetics Attila addressed the physical requirements that were placed on it, in a form which people would want in their homes.

Dimensions	**385x120mm**
Features	**High impact strength even at low temperatures**
	Good scratch resistance; Flame resistant
	Good stiffness and mechanical strength
	Low specific gravity; Easy to process
	Relative thermal index up to 176°F (80°C)
	Good dimensional stability at high temperatures
More	**www.rexite.it, www.geplastics.com**
	www.basf.de/plasticsportal, www.dow.com
Features	**Toys, automotive consoles, door panels, exterior grilles, domestic appliance housings, medical devices, business equipment, phone housings, building and construction products.**

Brutally effective

168

Machine washable

We no longer have to rely on rigid, or semi-rigid materials for our electronic products. ElekTex™ is a fabric that is conductive, intelligent, and responsive to touch, with the ability to process data. The material offers a soft, flexible, lightweight interface, which was previously only available with rigid materials.

Products made using ElekTex™ technology act in the same ways as conventional textiles in that they can be washed and worn. The fabrics make use of standard nylon or polyester with an electrical conductive coating. The potential for future electronic products that do not need to rely on a rigid panel to hold the electronics is massive. The freedom to create wearable technology where communications devices are built into the clothes we wear begins to blur the boundaries of technology. Technology will no longer be seen as a separate entity contained in a plastic box, but as an integral part of our surroundings.

Features	**Capable of switching and sensing technology**
	Can detect X-Y positioning
	Can be stitched and woven into garments
	No need for rigid circuitry
	Can be washed
	Soft and flexible
More	**www.elektex.com**
Applications	**Mobile communications, text interfacing, toys, car parts, healthcare, sports and leisurewear.**

**Conference phone
ElekTex™**

Make no mistake, polycarbonate is the hard man of plastic. It offers one of the highest impact resistances compared with any other plastic. It is many times stronger than glass and for this reason is used heavily in the glazing industry. However, it has its weaknesses. There are certain combinations of environments, temperature, and stress that can adversely affect it. When it is attacked by certain organic chemicals it can be susceptible to cracking.

Once you have taken this into account there are many additives that can be used to bolster its uses. Polycarbonate is available in a wide range of grades, such as UV stable, high-flow, glass-reinforced, flame resistant, water resistant, lubricity, high-optical clarity, and wear resistant. Depending on the production method used—injection molded, extruded, blow molded, or foamed—polycarbonate will have different properties, each process requiring a different grade. Kartell has used the plastic in a range of domestic products where strength is a critical factor.

Tough and clear

Dimensions	500x875x525mm
Features	**Outstanding impact resistance**
	Excellent optical clarity; Flame resistant
	Excellent dimensional stability even at even at high temperatures; Durable; Nontoxic
	Excellent range of colors; Easy to process
	Good heat resistance up to 257°F (125°C)
	UV stable
	Available as transparent, translucent, and opaque
	Recyclable (post-industrial and post-consumer)
More	**www.exatec.de, www. dsmep.com**
Applications	**Safety helmets, eyewear, architectural glazing, CDs and DVDs, kitchen containers, packaging, computer housings, automotive, cellphone housings, visors.**

La Mairie
Client: Kartell
Designer: Philippe Starck

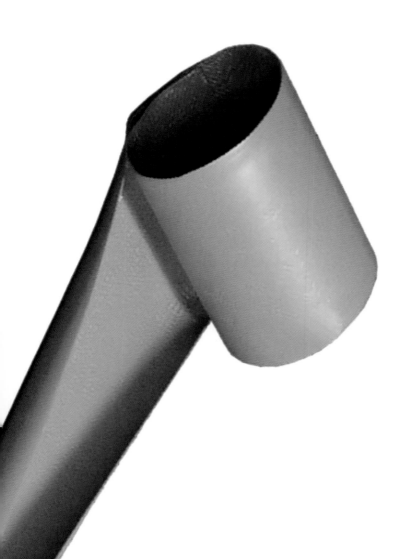

Rolatube™ has developed and patented a Bi-stable composite material that transforms from a flat strip in its rolled-up coil state, to tubular forms when it is pulled from its coil. Unlike a tape measure, which relies on the casing to contain the inherent tension, the Rolatube™ technology needs no outside force to hold it in either position, which is where the reference to Bi-stable comes in. The material is made from glass, aramid, or carbon fibers held within a thermoplastic matrix such as polypropylene or nylon. The choice of polymer is dictated by the end use—normally temperature conditions and chemical resistance—and has no effect on the ability of the product to bend. Color can be added to the polymer when required. Typically the formed shapes are tubes, which can be open or overlapped, or created to be less enclosed. These shapes can be rolled and unrolled thousands of times without any loss of performance.

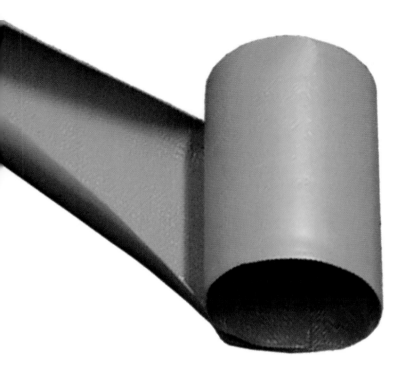

Flat to three-dimensional

Dimensions	**Tube diameters: 2–140mm**
Features	**Stable structure; Portable**
	High cycle life
	High strength-to-weight ratio; Bi-stable
	Easy to store; Easy to access
	Cost effective in terms of storage and transportation
More	**www.rolatube.com**
Applications	**Temporary communications masts or struts which can be rolled in or out many times, permanently installed structures such as pipes which need to be easily transported and stored, machines for deploying cameras, tools for remote operation in hazardous environments.**

173 Green Plastics

Naturally wearing

Features	**Superior strength**
	Natural fibers create a unique aesthetic
	Surface is enhanced with age, as with wood or leather
More	**www.studiorob.co.uk**
Applications	**Scratches, knocks, and chips are hidden by the richness of this naturally decorative material. This makes it suitable for anything that has a lot of "people contact," including flooring and furniture, and personal products, such as briefcases.**

Designer Rob Thompson has contributed to the evolution of plastics with his "material memories" project. Dealing with the visible signs of age on a product's surface, he has looked at how composite materials can be given the capacity to enhance emotional bonding between product and user.

He explains, "I combined plastic with natural fiber-based materials such as straw, wood shavings, feathers, hemp, and recycled newspaper. This resulted in new and exciting composites that utilize the versatile and moldable qualities of synthetic materials with the ageing, aesthetic qualities of natural fibers."

There are many ways in which these products can be adapted in the future. The look of the material will change as different forms of recycled paper are added, such as used billboards. As the paper and typefaces of newspapers change, so will the composite.

The real benefit of these composites and products is that they look to the future, as opposed to being nostalgic. They are sensitive to our desire for material memories in the fast-developing and transient world of the commodities that surround us.

Material Memories Stools
Designer: Rob Thompson

Stars in stripes

My definition of "new materials" includes those that have been given new potential by being employed in new territories. It's always exciting to talk about the use of completely new substances and technologies, but there is as much invention and ingenuity in finding new applications for an old substance as there is in developing a new one. This discussion of reuse is even more important than the area of emerging technologies and materials because it includes sustainability.

Cellulose acetate (CA) has two of these criteria: the first lies in the fact that cellulose is starch and, as a result, is derived from a rapidly renewable source rather than the oil-based feedstock from which most other polymers are derived. Second, although it is an old material, it is being given a new lease of life in the design industry.

Originally a replacement for celluloid—the trade name for cellulose nitrate—due to its lower burning rate, CA has been used since the 1930s for a variety of products. As one of the oldest forms of mass-producible plastics, it has been superseded by many newer advances. However, the Collective Vision exploration by designers at IDEO resurrects the potential of this material. Using two of Eastman Chemical's staple materials—copolyester and cellulose—the concepts within this collection highlight the contemporary benefits of a material that is ancient in terms of plastics.

Features	
	Warm to the skin
	Very tough
	Derived from a renewable source
	Self-polishing
	Available in intense or translucent colors
	Tactile surface
	Can be worked or polished by hand
	Easily molded
More	**www.ideo.com**
	www.eastman.com
Applications	**Toothbrushes, tool handles, hairclips, cutlery handles, toys, playing cards, dice, screwdriver handles, goggles.**

Collective Vision Project
Designers: Martin Bone, Markus Diebel, Kara Johnson, Thomas Overthun, Pontus Wahlgren, and Rico Zorkendorfer at IDEO
Client: Eastman Chemicals

Form-hugging

Industrial netting is a highly underrated semiformed material. It has many advantages: it is lightweight, strong, and uses very little material.

In terms of forming, it is extruded into tubes. As with many types of netting, the rhomboidal structure allows for a natural ability of the net when stretched to conform to the most economical shape, wrapping and hugging itself around items of any shape.

In this packaging design, the netting was used to overcome the problem of how to enclose a set of large, domestic cleaning products in a package that was not excessive in scale, cost, or materials. The products' retail price was a major issue, as these items were designed to appeal to people setting up their first home. The simple color and aesthetics of the products were also selling points,

as was the ability to see them in the package. Traditional board materials were rejected due to the cost and quantity of material that would have been needed for each set. However, the combination of the cardboard tray and polypropylene netting provided a strong, cheap, and transparent alternative that allowed for branding, and which also allowed for an integral handle to carry the products with.

Features	**Contents are exposed but still protected**
	Good strength-to-weight ratio
	Can fit any form
	Available in a range of diameters
More	**www.tenax.net**
Applications	**Nets for industrial and horticultural applications, including Christmas-tree netting, and nets for pallet loads. Other nets are used for protecting industrial components, for packaging of fruit and vegetables, toys, and even as sponge nets.**

John Lewis
Essentials
Spring clean

Dustpan & brush
13.5 litre Bucket
Window Blade
Scrubbing brush
Cleaning cloth

Spring clean

Dustpan & brush
13.5 litre bucket
Window blade
Scrubbing brush
Cleaning cloth

**Packaging for Essentials
cleaning products
Designers: Pearce Marchbank
and Chris Lefteri
Client: John Lewis Partnership**

Compostable

Along with nanocomposites, environmentally friendly products are one of the fastest-growing areas within plastics. Bioplastics are an aspect of this movement toward environmental credibility. They provide a perfect cycle of materials. The cycle starts with cornstarch. This is transformed into pellets, processed into products, used by consumers, and then returned to the ground without releasing pollutants.

Mater-Bi™ is one such cornstarch-based bioplastic, developed by Novamont. It is a plastic derived from a rapidly renewable source, and is both biodegradable and compostable.

In this application for a new type of eating utensil, the economy of material is also applied to the economy of function: the spoon and fork are combined in the same product. Within the scale and thin wall section, the material is slightly springy and has a lustrous tactile quality—it feels more like a natural material than a traditional plastic high-sheen product. Although it has this slightly soft feel, it is also pretty tough, which has led to one of its many other applications: dog chews!

Moscardino disposable
spoon/fork made from
Mater-Bi™ plastic
Designers: Matteo Ragni and
Giulio Iacchetti
Manufacturer: Pandora Design

Dimensions	**80x40mm**
Features	**Completely biodegradable in different environments**
	Compostable in soil, fresh water, and salt water
	Easy to form using traditional plastic techniques
	Printable using normal inks and printing techniques without the need for crown treatment
	Intrinsically antistatic; Sterilized using gamma rays
	Can incorporate masterbatches
More	**www.materbi.com; www.pandoradesign.it**
Applications	**Food packaging, toys, pens, Q tips, diapers, catering products, compost bags, dog chews, biodegradable shopping bags, extruded nets for food packaging, kitchen paper rolls, stationery items such as rulers and pencil sharpeners. Mater-Bi™ can also be converted to foams.**

182

Soluble packaging

One of the disadvantages of plastics is that they have an image problem, particularly in terms of environmental friendliness. However, there are many case studies of new materials that are overcoming the major issue of waste disposal. One of the hottest topics in discussions about environmental issues is materials that degrade, whether through solubility, biodegradation, or photodegradation.

Polyvinyl alcohol (PVA) has been around for some time, and today is commonly seen in the form of detergent dispensers for washing machines. But designers have yet to embrace the possibilities of this valuable technology whereby products dissolve in water, having performed their primary function, and leave nothing behind.

Although most of the existing applications are in packaging, there is a constant stream of new developments within water-soluble and other degradable materials. There is no reason why they can't be used for injection-moldable or extruded products.

This image of cradlewrap illustrates an application for PVA as a packaging material. It combines a highly impact-resistant structure with a PVA material, which either dissolves in water or is compostable. Taking less than a minute to dissolve in warm tap water, it disintegrates from a thin plastic material to a slippery gel that consists of nothing but carbon dioxide and water.

CradleWrap water soluble packing material

Features	Biodegradable; Environmentally sound
	Nonhazardous
	Solubility can be controlled by hot or cold water
	Good resistance to chemicals
	Nontoxic residue after it dissolves
	Can offer good degree of transparency
	Good tensile strength and elasticity
	Printable
	Offers user-controllable solubility
More	www.amtrexintl.com
	www.aquasol-ltd.com
	www.stanelco.devisland.net
	www.stanelcoplc.com
Applications	Applications range from the soap containers for washing machines to edible films. Industrial uses include pharmaceuticals, washaway labels, hospital laundry bags where contaminated clothes can be disposed of without human contact, and public toilet seat protectors. It is also being explored as an alternative to traditional gelatin-based pill capsules, veterinary applications, and plant pesticide capsules that dissolve to release the pesticide into the soil.

The technology that enables us to manufacture products has developed over thousands of years, allowing evolutions of new methods and techniques and the introduction of completely new ways to make our objects quicker, cheaper, and in larger volumes. It is only recently that we have had to consider the other side of the coin, which is what happens when we throw these objects away. It is the realization that we have become too good at making things faster and cheaper that has prompted research into ways in which materials can have their lives extended—or eradicated.

Wash it away

At the very heart of the definition of plastics is the ability of materials to be easily transformed from one state, usually liquid, to another. In virtually all cases, this transition is used to make parts. Plantic® demonstrates the increasing number of applications where the process of transformation is reversed and is used to destroy and safely dispose of the product. Plantic® is as versatile as traditional plastics; it also looks and feels the same. The difference lies in the fact that Plantic® is made from starch, and, importantly, it dissolves in water.

The makers, Plantic Technologies, relate the biodegradability rate of the plastic with that of household food scraps. Plantic® can be put into the garden composting heap or simply thrown in your trashcan.

Features	**Biodegradable**
	Environmentally sound
	Nonhazardous
	Nontoxic residue after it dissolves
More	**www.plantic.com.au**
Applications	**A large market for Plantic® appears to be for trays in the confectionery industry. However, Plantic® can be used to injection mold just about anything, from children's toys to car parts.**

Chocolates tray made from Plantic water-soluble plastic

Sample of Natraplast® wood-plastic composite

The idea of combining plastics and wood fibers is not new. However, with our urgent need to reexamine how we use our resources, and with research into sustainable materials and composites, such materials are seeing a massive renewal of interest.

There are a number of benefits to using wood-plastic composites, the main one being that they combine the workability of timber with the processability of plastics. They can be injection molded, rotationally molded, and, more popularly, extruded. This can be achieved using a number of plastics, including polystyrene, polyethylene, and polypropylene.

Wood-plastic composites also reduce the amount of raw plastic material that is required to produce a component. They also allow for a reduction in cycle times for injection molding due to the part cooling faster and having less shrinkage (and therefore higher tolerances).

Natraplast® is one of the many products that combine these two materials. It is a material that bridges plastic mass production and handworking, while also providing an oaty, natural surface alternative to the traditional plastic surface aesthetic.

Features (compared with wood)	**Increases dimensional stability**
	Hard; Abrasion resistant
	Good compressive strength
	Rot resistant
	Low moisture absorption
Features (compared with plastic)	**Strength; Stiffness**
	Impact resistant
	Reduces cycle time for injection molding; cools down faster
	Less shrinkage on the final product, therefore high tolerances
More	**www.wtl-int.com**
	www.hackwellgroup.co.uk
Applications	**Window frames, decking, sheet panels, pipes, tubes, buckets, fittings, bowls.**

Wood + plastic

A range of recycled plastic materials made from a variety of products including cellphones, rain boots, dolls, CDs, and water bottles

All that jazz

Dimensions	**Sheet sizes from 1,200x800mm to 3,000x1,500mm. Thickness from 2mm–25mm**
Features	**Made from recycled material**
	Recognizable and powerful aesthetic
	Low fabrication costs
	Available in a range of thicknesses
More	**www.smile-plastics.co.uk**
Applications	**Guitar bodies, kitchen worktops and doors, chairs, tables, exterior and interior screens.**

The plastics recycling industry has been going for about 50 years. Initially the motivation to recycle was purely commercial, with companies looking for ways to reuse waste materials. In terms of the end results, the outcome was not that exciting, with the recycled materials being hidden behind bland, gray, almost embarrassed surfaces. By setting up Smile Plastics, Colin Williamson saw the opportunity to reinterpret the recycling process by making it a highly visible feature of the final material. Based on the "jazz" effect (a pattern that was born out of molders experimenting with leftover virgin plastics during the molding process), Williamson saw the potential of this decorative accident to create a material that wore its recycling badge on its sleeve.

The specks of discarded and shredded products clearly visible in the surface of these sheet materials is reminiscent of compacted cars, or the effect of someone taking a section of a compressed landfill site. The visible history of the discarded products compacted into the surface tells the story of the material and of the times, mentally closing the loop in terms of what happens to the material once it is recycled.

This material makes people far more willing to enter into recycling schemes because they can see the benefit. The aesthetic of discarded items, such as detergent bottles, changes as the discarded items change (with recent additions including cellphones), and these are compressed together into sheets. Depending on the origin of the virgin material the various products can have tactile qualities that range from soft and supple to hard and resilient.

As environmental issues become increasingly mainstream, so too are the related products available to consumers. Products and services are emerging that combine aesthetic pleasure with a measure of ethical fulfillment.

This project looks at how one of the most banal object typologies could merge with an environmental activity to produce a new hybrid. This watering can-cum-trashcan is based on the observation that a watering can often becomes the place in the home where we store and reuse waste water: tea and coffee; water from boiling or steaming; water from vases of flowers; rainwater, and so on—all of which is good for our plants.

The project addresses the question of what a product might look like if it was to be both liquid trashcan and watering can. The unique aesthetic is driven by its inviting, flared spout, which embraces this new function.

Can the can

Dimensions	**260x275x405mm**
Features	**Waxy; Easy to mold**
	Tough at low temperatures
	Low cost
	Flexible
	Good chemical resistance
More	**hugojamson@hotmail.com**
	www.rotomolding.org
Applications	**Toys, chemical drums, household and kitchenware, cable insulation, carrier bags, automobile fuel tanks, furniture, Tupperware.**

Watering can
Designer: Hugo Jamson

Plastic from corn

"Your food comes from nature; so does your container," proclaims the NatureWorks® website. NatureWorks® PLA is a technology based on the ability to extract starch from corn and other plants to make polyactide (PLA) polymer. Once the corn has been milled, the starch that is present is separated from the raw material. Unrefined dextrose is produced from this starch. The dextrose is then turned into lactic acid, using a similar process to that for making wine and beer. This dextrose is the same lactic acid that is found in food additives and also in human muscle tissue. Then, through a special condensation process, a cyclic intermediate dimer, also known as lactide, is formed. The lactide, which is the monomer, is purified through vacuum distillation. The process is completed by polymerization, which happens through a solvent-free melt process.

The ultimate aim of the manufacturer of NatureWorks®, Cargill Dow, is to produce PLA more cheaply than PET resin and eventually become a substitute for polyethylene.

The products have all the elements you would expect of a packaging material, with high clarity and hinges. To all intents, it would be indistinguishable from a standard product. However, apart from the injection-molded products, PLA can be modified to produce a variety of applications such as fibers, foams, emulsions, and chemical intermediaries.

Features	Comes from an annually renewable source
	Stiffness and processing temperatures similar to polyolefin resins
	Compostable; Low odor
	Good clarity; Good surface finish
More	www.natureworksllc.com
Applications	Blow-molded bottles, water-based emulsions, clothing, carpet tiles, rigid thermoformed food and beverage containers, diapers, adhesives, geo textiles.

Cup and fork made from
Naturework® PLA

You will need:
- Polyethylene resin
- A pinch of additive
- Extruding machine
- Organic kitchen/garden waste

What to do:
- Take a large container and mix together the polyethylene resin and a low dose of additives.
- Place the mix in your film-extruding machine, and run off as many bags as you think you will need for the waste in your kitchen and garden. Separate the bags and fill with your garden refuse. Once you have filled your bags place them in a commercial compost heap (windrow system). After about three months the bag has vanished (apart from minute quantities of carbon dioxide and water) and you should have a heap of compost.

Not only can this product totally degrade, but the time can be set for it to disappear as well. A unique property for a plastic bag, it can have a life for as long as you require it. So a bag can be designed to last for two to five years, or only a few months.

Symphony Environmental uses a technology known as EPIs®, TDPA™ (Totally Degradable Compostable Additive). This process uses a small percentage of the additive, which can be combined with polyethylene or polypropylene resins. The additive used does not affect the properties of the finished film. The degradation process, which is affected by light, heat, and stress (pulling and tearing), begins as soon as the material goes into use.

Features	**Fully degradable**
	Relatively low cost
	Good chemical resistance
	Easy to process
	Polyethylenes are available in a number of physical grades (LDPE, HDPE, MDPE)
More	**www.symphonyplastics.co.uk**
	www.degradable.net
Applications	**Packaging, refuse sacks, food produce bags, food freezer bags, carrier bags.**

No residue

Plastic can be used in combination with other materials to form new interesting composites. Old jeans, retired bank notes, and coconut coir are some of the fillers used by Grot in their plastic recipes. The addition of these materials challenges notions of composites being high-tech like carbon or glass fiber.

Grot Global Resource Technology started to produce composite materials offering a natural alternative to virgin, recycled, mineral, or glass-filled thermoplastics. They produce a range of polymers, which allow for an assortment of natural fibers to be added to them. From this basis a range of products for a variety of applications can be made using different production methods, including extrusion, injection molding, compression molding, and blow molding.

The materials are made by melt-blending natural fibers with a range of thermoplastics. The physical and visual qualities of the final composite are determined by the natural fiber selected, for which Grot offer certain recommendations. If you are looking for a strong visual quality they recommend polypropylene mixed with either rice hulls, pine wood dust, coconut coir, or sisal as the best combination. If it's tensile strength you're after they can recommend kenaf (mesta), jute, hemp, flax, and Kraft wood fiber (not sawdust).

Old jeans

Features	**Natural appearance**
	Low cost: less than the base resin
	Fully and easily recyclable; Easy to color
	Reduced molding cycle time, up to 30%
	Nonabrasive to machinery; Low mold shrinkage
	Low thermal expansion coefficient
	High tensile and flex modulus: up to 5 x base resin
	Lower processing energy requirements
More	**www.execpc.com/~grot/index.htm**
Applications	**Automobile interiors, construction products, office products, furniture, storage containers, window and picture frames, food service trays, fan housings and blades, toys.**

Rags to riches

Textile designer Luisa Cervese uses many different materials in her fun and elegant handbags, totes, and cushions. While working as a textile researcher for a major textile company, Cervese noticed the amount of textile offcuts that just got thrown away. This waste inspired her to start experimenting by combining textile waste with plastics of different properties. Using different types of plastic means that each batch of material requires a different form of manufacture thus leading to an array of different results and unique products.

Cervese's aim was to create products that were simple yet unique and which involve the minimum amount of waste. The quality of the plastic is important but each plastic can be chosen to suit the final product. Silk polyurethane can be rolled very thin and combines well with the waste to produce a material ideal for bags and raincoats. Not only does it give the products their individuality, but it also provides durability, waterproofing, and structure.

Features	**Low material costs**
	Extremely durable; Strong
	Highly flexible
	Good water resistance
More	**www.riedizioni.com**
Applications	**Handbags, purses, clothing, placemats, cushions.**

Riedizioni
Designer: Luisa Cervese

Metamorphosis

Dimensions	**140x8mm**
Features	**Made from recycled material**
	Low cost
	Requires less energy to convert the material than to use virgin polystyrene
	High visible appeal for the benefits of recycling
More	**www.save-a-cup.co.uk**
	www.re-markable.com
Applications	**Stationery and office equipment.**

The Save-a-Cup scheme was
established as a nonprofit company
by vending, foodservice, and plastics
industries to collect the millions of
vending cups thrown away every week.
The use of a single material in the initial
production and the captive environment
in which they are used allows for
easy collection.

Participating organizations use special
collectors, designed to condense up to
480 cups, with a facility to pour off any
liquid. The cups are discharged into
polyethylene sacks for regular collection
by a Save-a-Cup vehicle for delivery to
the reprocessing operation.

During reprocessing, contaminants
are removed before the material is
converted into dry flakes, or farther
processed into pellets suitable for
wide-ranging applications.

Remarkable is dedicated to giving
second life to the thousands of tonnes
of waste produced every day. As well as
plastic cups, they also produce products
from food and drinks containers, paper,
and car tires. The unique Millenium
Pencils are each made from one
recycled polystyrene vending cup.

**Millennium Pencil
Designers: Remarkable Pencils**

201 Production Plastics

Big moldings

New techniques are being developed all the time to help convert both new and existing materials into new and exciting forms. There are layers of methods split and divided by material families; processes that are specific to industries; and processes within processes. However, at the top of the knowledge tree for designers is injection molding. Within it there are various subcategories, one of which is gas-injection molding.

The difference between gas-injection molding and injection molding is that at the stage where molten plastic is injected into the mold, gas is also introduced, with the result that plastic is forced against the walls of the mold until the plastic has cooled. This has several advantages over conventional injection molding. First, products in conventional molding require a solid section of plastic, which is fine for thin wall thicknesses, but for large-scale, thick sections, products become heavy and require a lot of material. Gas-injection molding, however, allows for parts to be made with varying wall thicknesses and hollow sections filled with air. The shrinkage and sink marks that are common in injection moldings are eliminated due to the even distribution of pressure within the mold, which also results in greater surface definition.

Magis has years of experience in producing plastic design-led products, and it uses gas-injection molding on some of its large-scale pieces of furniture. This range of chairs is typical of the process.

**Cinecitta: chair made from glass-filled polypropylene with seat and back in waterproof nylon
Designer: Enzo Mari**

Dimensions	**560x820mm**
Features	**Uses less material**
	Reduced cycle times
	Allows for components to be made with variable wall thickness
	Reduced weight
	Cost-effective
	Less sink marking
	Greater surface definition
More	**www.gasinjection.com**
	www.magisdesign.com
Applications	**If you think of the big plastic garden furniture available from garden centers, the chances are they have been made by gas-injection molding. However, virtually all moldable parts can be gas-injection molded, including coat hangers, vacuum cleaner bases, and wing-mirror housings. External gas-injection molding is often used for components with large surface areas, such as auto body panels, furniture, and refrigerators.**

Mass customization

Dimensions	**360x280x60mm**
Features	**Allows for rapid response to fashion**
	Can provide enhanced functional surface
	Cost-effective
	Enhances branding possibilities
More	**www.inclosia.com**
	www.tulip-ego.com
	www.mvgdesign.us
Applications	**Cellphones, PDAs, computer peripherals.**

The rapid growth of the personal technology area has allowed designers to play with new functions and applications for new typologies. All manner of music, information, organization, and communication products used to be exclusively made from molded standard ABS (acrylonitrile butadiene styrene), derived from a global visual identity. But now, with the ability to incorporate softer materials into the sphere of mass production, design has been liberated to create new visual languages for products and can offer regional and personal ranges with the addition of new skins.

Inclosia Solutions has developed a patented technology, the EXO™ overmolding system, which allows materials such as wood, leather, metals, and fabrics to be incorporated into plastic moldings. The technology enables manufacturers to quickly and cost-effectively change surface designs and apply functional and aesthetic decoration to a range of products.

Based on a multistage process where the skin is inserted into the mold and plastic injected over it, the technology uses a full range of sheet materials to create aesthetic and functional qualities with a high-volume, mass-market product. Inclosia opens the door for technology to be dressed in soft, tactile, and scented woods and leathers, or the cold, hard surface of aluminum.

Tulip E-Go Laptop
Designer: Marcel van Galen
Client: Tulip Computers

Personal mass production

Provista® is a brand of PETG (polyethylene terephthalate glycol) copolyester from Eastman Chemicals. It was developed for use in extrusions that required optical clarity, toughness, and flexibility. All these properties are evident in Tom Dixon's "Fresh Fat" range of products.

What makes this project especially interesting is the combination of a high-volume, mass-production process, and the interpretation of plastic as a handmade craft project. There are many examples of designers using plastic in a craft-like process, but here Tom Dixon uses a high-volume machine as his tool. This unorthodox approach contradicts preconceived notions of plastic as the material of mass production.

The project provides a new opportunity for combining machine and hand production, allowing for the personalization of a mass-production process. In its tangled, spaghetti-like form, it expresses the simple reason why plastic is so good at the job of forming shapes. When heated, this pliable, gooey material takes on whatever shape contains it and it stays that way when it cools.

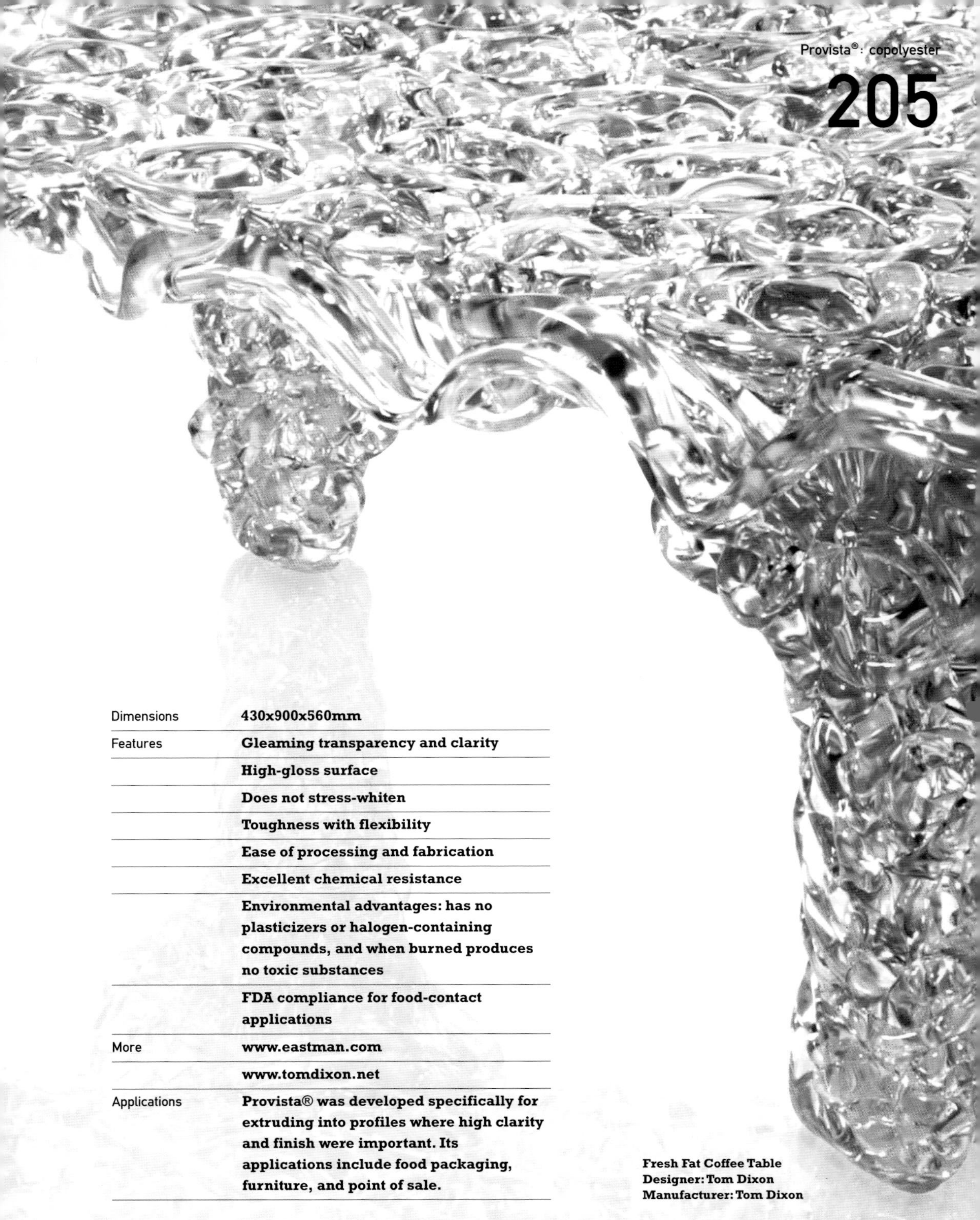

Dimensions	**430x900x560mm**
Features	**Gleaming transparency and clarity**
	High-gloss surface
	Does not stress-whiten
	Toughness with flexibility
	Ease of processing and fabrication
	Excellent chemical resistance
	Environmental advantages: has no plasticizers or halogen-containing compounds, and when burned produces no toxic substances
	FDA compliance for food-contact applications
More	**www.eastman.com**
	www.tomdixon.net
Applications	**Provista® was developed specifically for extruding into profiles where high clarity and finish were important. Its applications include food packaging, furniture, and point of sale.**

**Fresh Fat Coffee Table
Designer: Tom Dixon
Manufacturer: Tom Dixon**

Rubber-cut fabrics
Designer: Lauren Moriarty

3D fabrics

With an emphasis on the constant development of new ways to work with materials, designer Lauren Moriarty has mixed contemporary textiles with product design to create a fresh and original approach. Combining a foam material and laser cutting, Moriarty has built a range of patterns that explores the use of rubber and plastics to create a modern take on traditional textile techniques.

She says: "Many of the pieces I produce are laser-cut before being molded into shape. The advantage of laser-cutting is the very intricate detail that can be achieved. The cut layers are constructed into three-dimensional pieces and take the form of lighting, cushions, and interior cubes. These three-dimensional 'fabrics' are squashable and have great tactile appeal. The single-layer fabrics relate to the patterns found in lace and constructed textiles, and address the aim of finding new ways to explore textile design using materials not often associated with the subject."

Moriarty's approach to experimentation and the resulting flexible, soft, semi-organic, open-cell foam structures and flat patterns define a new application for foams.

Dimensions	**2x500x1,000mm**
Features	**Lightweight; Flexible**
	Can be produced in a range of materials
	Cushioning
More	**www.laurenmoriarty.co.uk**
Applications	**Cushions, lighting, interior paneling.**

Reinventing jewelry

Dimensions	**230x120mm**
Features	**Can be heat-welded, ultrasonically welded, riveted, stitched, and embossed**
	Easy and versatile processing
	Excellent resistance to chemicals
	Excellent live hinge potential
	Low water absorption and permeability to water vapor
	Recyclable
	Very cheap tooling
	Manual assembly process
	High print adhesion
	Virtually impossible to tear
	Low density
More	**www.barbara-schmidt-schmuck.de**
Applications	**Packaging, stationery, table mats, folio cases, furniture, lighting.**

This project is a wonderful combination of material and production, and a great example of a cross–referencing of products. Combining high- and low-value objects, the Postcardring© brings a new meaning to the whole concept of value.

The rings can be sent in an envelope and brought to life by popping out the ring from its die-cut postcard and hooking the ends together to wrap it around the finger. The project encompasses a range of sheet materials and colors from which the rings can be ordered. Apart from them being a completely new expression of jewelry, the products make a clever connection between low-tech die-cutting technology and do-it-yourself assembly.

Objects to go

Dimensions	**730x440x440mm**
Features	**Virtually limitless possibilities of shapes**
	Available in a range of materials
	Low capital investment
More	**www.patrickjouin.com**
	www.materialise.com
Applications	**Car manufacturers, engineers, designers, and architects use stereo lithography to produce prototypes and concept models. In manufacturing it is used to create patterns and masters for melds and short run final products. Surgeons have also begun to use this technology to recreate affected anatomy in preparation for complicated operations.**

Rapid prototyping is changing the world of production, as it allows for previously impossible forms to be produced as multiples. Originally, rapid prototyping was a process used to develop samples quickly, but it is now being pushed outside of this role into a much broader way of making objects. The tool provides freedom from the constraints of the manufacturing process to offer a new world of possible objects.

There is an ever-increasing number of methods within this manufacturing family. Most common types use lasers and photosensitive resin for stereolithography—laminated paper built up in layers and ink-jet. This project uses a range of powder and liquid polymers to create the various pieces from inputted designs.

In a process that is so forward-looking, there is nevertheless a reference to the past in the sense that objects are created from solid materials in a one-off. This is one of the most intriguing areas to watch, where complex structures are slowly brought to life from a solid mass over a period of a hours. Objects reveal themselves like magic.

Solid chair
Designer: Patrick Jouin
Manufacturer: 3D Systems

The pull of the new

In principle, pultrusions are similar to extrusions, but instead of pushing doughy plastic through a die, the plastic is pulled, taking with it fibers to act as reinforcement. It is here that the similarity ends. Whereas extrusions are used for low-temp metals and plastics to form a continuous length of the same shape, pultrusions make the same type of shape, but instead create high-strength and highly rigid profiles.

Pultrusions provide another example of plastics competing with metals. The resultant forms offer super rigidity, with an 80–75 percent weight reduction on steel and 30 percent on aluminum, as well as a greater dimensional stability than these metals.

Increasing the physical properties for both engineering and design applications, pultruded plastics offer the toughness of metals with the advantages of low weight and corrosion resistance. They are extremely dense and hard; they feel more like metal than plastic and "clank" like a piece of metal when you knock them. They can also be colored without the problem of chipping. Surface decoration can be applied to mimic grain and other textures. As you would expect from plastics, pultruded plastics are also nonconductive, which makes them an ideal material for electricians' ladders.

Dimensions	**Profiles range from 1–250mm diameter**
Features	**Highly rigid; Colorable; Strong**
	Lightweight; Nonconductive
	Corrosion resistant
	Good dimensional stability
More	**www.pultruders.com**
	www.acmanet.org
	www.fibreforce.co.uk
Applications	**As an alternative to metal, pultrusions are used for permanent and temporary structural components for industrial plants; vandal-resistant indoor and outdoor public furniture, funfairs, and exhibition stands. Smaller-scale applications include electrically insulated ladders, ski poles, racket handles, fishing rods, and bicycle frames. Perhaps more surprisingly, pultrusions have a similar resonance to certain woods, which has led to them replacing hard wood frames in xylophones.**

The Eglu chicken coop, made by Omlet, is made from rotational-molded polyethylene. This material is similar to PVC in the volume of its consumption worldwide and its availability in an extensive range of varieties. Some formulas of polyethylene are bendable and supple, while others are rigid; some are highly resistant to breaking, whereas others are easily broken. However, as a family, polyethylenes are characterized by chemical resistance and toughness. High-density polyethylene (HDPE) is used in the Eglu because of its stiffness and strength.

The Eglu is a wonderful advert for rotational molding in polyethylene. The bright, contemporary colors and large moldings are the perfect opportunity to show one of the key advantages of this prolific partnership of material and molding technique.

Dimensions	**700x800x800mm**
Features	**Waxy; Easy to mold**
	Tough at low temperatures
	Low cost; Flexible
	Good chemical resistance
More	**www.omlet.co.uk**
Applications	**Chemical drums, toys, household and kitchenware, cable insulation, carrier bags, car fuel tanks, furniture, Tupperware.**

Chicken architecture

Eglu chicken coop
Designers: James Tuthill,
Johannes Paul, Simon Nichols,
and William Windham
Manufacturer: Omlet

217 Familiar

The design and production of many sporting products have used the science of materials to their fullest: TPEs for diving fins, composites in racket sports, aminos in bowls. The intelligent dimpled surface of a golf ball is designed to affect its flight and height when it is propelled at 150mph down the fairway.

Originally made of feathers wrapped in a leather skin, the outer skin of modern golf balls is made from a high-impact, cut-resistant polyethylene. Anyone who has ever dissected a golf ball will know that behind the skin you will often find a tight bundle of elastic bands, over which the polyethylene is injection molded. The core is held in place in the mold by pins, which are retracted just before the process is complete. The seam is then cut and sanded off, followed by a coat of varnish.

Dimensions	**Diameter 41mm**
Features	**High melt strength**
	Outstanding impact toughness
	Abrasion, scuff, and chemical resistant
	Good transparency and clarity
	Direct adhesion to metal, glass, and natural fibers by heat lamination
	Direct adhesion of epoxy and polyurethane finishes
More	**www.dupont.com/industrial-polymers/surlyn**
Applications	**Door handles, toys, hockey helmets, perfume bottles, footwear, body boards, ten-pin bowling pins, tool handles.**

Tough skin

Maxfli
Client: Dunlop
Designer: Dunlop Slazenger
International R&D Team

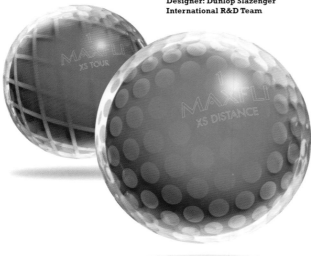

**Flexboard
Designer: Man and
Machine Inc.**

A new gesture

Dimensions	**499x175x7mm; weight 700g**
Features	**Excellent tear strength**
	Good chemical resistance
	Outstanding flex life, cut and scratch resistance
	Flexible; High elasticity; Good color range
	Wide range of physical forms and mechanical properties
More	**www.mmits.com**
Applications	**Sheeting, car fenders, bladders, fuel line tubing, packaging material, car body moldings.**

It's soft and flexible, and it bends and twists like rubber. The Flexboard is manufactured from polyurethane foam, an ideal material for this application because of its oil and solvent resistance. It can also be cast in a mold. Keys are laser-etched to save the cost of retooling for different languages. The keyboard stays flexible due to a series of rigid pieces of printed circuit board rather than a flexible PCB.

Since it can be manufactured either in rigid or flexible form, polyurethane caters for a wide field of applications. Soft-foamed polyurethane is used for cushions, mattresses, and trims. Hard polyurethane is employed in the automotive, construction, and furniture industries, where it is highly valued as a material with exceptionally good thermal and acoustic insulation properties.

Takes the knocks

Dimensions	**Diameter 216mm**
Features	**Good impact strength; Excellent hardness**
	Good surface finish; Good stiffness
	Excellent dimensional stability
	Low friction; Excellent resistance to chemicals
	Recyclable (PET is one of the most recycled plastic resins)
More	**www.columbia300.com**
Applications	**Soft drink bottles and food packaging.**

Modern bowling began in the early nineteenth century with balls originally made from the hardwood lignum vitae until the 1960s when polyester became an ideal replacement.

There are many functions that these bowling balls needed to satisfy above being hard-wearing. The bowling alley is a demanding environment with balls weighing from 8lb to 16lb and the industry dictating that all balls should have a consistant Shore hardness of 73. Each ball contains a variety of fillers for the different weights, from heamatite for heavy density to glass micro balloons for the lighter balls. The cores are then cast in polyester resin within a steel mold from which they emerge with a rough surface. These are then turned and

ground into a sphere. Holes are drilled according to the user's grip after purchase. PETs are one of two main polyesters—the other being polybutylene terephthalate (PBT)—that compete with nylons. As well as being used in the textile industry their other main household application is in carbonated drink bottles.

With continual hitting speeds of 14mph, pins need to withstand constant knocking, which they manage by having a wooden core coated with polyethylene resin.

Bowling balls
Brunswick

Features	**High impact resistance; Scratch resistant**
	Very high gloss; Easy to color
	Excellent resistance to chemicals
	Heat resistant; Odor free
	Stain and fire resistant
	Good electrical insulation
	Limited production methods
More	**www.perstorp.com**
Applications	**Handles, fan housings, circuit breakers, buttons, dinnerware, plastic laminates, ashtrays.**

A beautiful surface

Like the bowling ball, the billiard ball is a product that needs high-impact resistance. For a speed of 0 to over 30km/h in less than one second, and a friction temperature of 482°F (250°C), it has to be made from a hard material. It has to be scratch resistant and resistant to chipping. The longer it holds its shiny surface the better the play and the less harm it can do to your baize.

Billiard balls are generally made from either melamine or polyester resin. Melamine resins were the first synthetic plastics to be used in mass production, and due to their excellent electrical insulation properties have been used in housing for electrical products. With similar properties to phenolic resins they are more appropriate for billiard and bowling balls due to their ability to easily absorb bright-colored dyes.

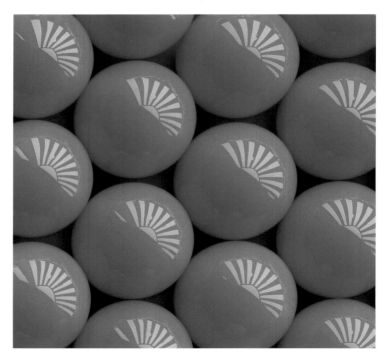

Aramith billiard ball

Good value

Dimensions	**From 5 to 300mm**
Features	**Low cost; Low shrinkage rate**
	Easy to mold and process; Easy to color
	Good transparency; Excellent adhesion
	Very low water moisture absorption
	High melt flow; Nontoxic
	Good dimensional stability; Recyclable
More	**www.huntsman.com, www.atofina.com**
Applications	**Fridge compartments, food packaging, audio equipment, coat hangers.**

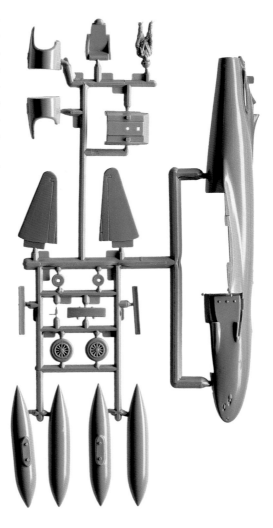

Anyone who has ever made an Airfix model is familiar with this particular plastic. The glue virtually welds two pieces of plastic together. Those intricate details are so precise you could see the smile on the aircraft pilot's face. The whole box was an illustration of a method of plastic production. Developed in 1939 by Nicholas Kove as a promotional tool for Fergasen, the first Airfix self-assembly model was produced in 1949.

The use of high-impact polystyrene provides a balance between cost of materials such as ABS, which can just as easily be injection molded and a material which can give the high definition needed in the intricate details of the parts. It has a stiff structure with relatively thin wall thicknesses and good adhesion allowing easy gluing and painting.

Lockheed F-80C
Client: Airfix
Designer: Nicholas Kove

Eiffel Tower Jelly
Designer: Patrick Cox

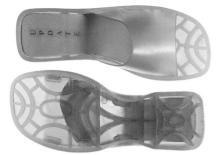

New form

Features	**Versatile; Easy to color; Cost-effective**
	Additives can give it a large range of properties
	Good resistance to chemicals; Easy to process
	Good corrosion and stain resistance
	Excellent outdoor performance; Good rigidity
More	**www.grendene.co.br**
Applications	**Packaging, dip molding, drain pipes, raincoats, domestic appliances, credit cards, car interiors.**

These shoes utilize the molding and color potential of plastics to create a new visual language for footwear. These objects are fascinating in their own right. The visible structure that provides a series of translucent windows is a great example of the mundane and everyday function of a pair of shoes made visible and highly decorative.

Although PVC is not the hardest wearing of materials it is a good compromise between strength, softness, and cost. Each shoe is expected to last two to three years with regular use.

The shoes are generally molded in two parts. In the case of the Eiffel Tower Jelly, the heel and sole are made from a single molding with the upper part glued separately. The heel is usually made from a harder grade of PVC and the upper from a softer grade. The water is then injected into the heal with a syringe. To stop the water from going green, it is treated with an antibacterial agent. The hole is then sealed up.

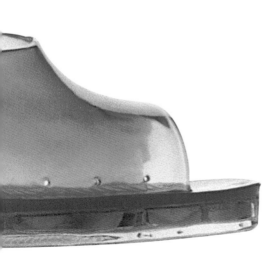

Urea is defined as "a substance found in mammalian urine" so what a perfect match of material with function that it should be used as a toilet seat. As a thermoset material it was one of the first materials to give Bakelite the shoulder, because unlike Bakelite it could be molded and produced in any color. Produced by heating urea and formaldehyde, it belongs to the family of organic polymers.

Because of its heavy weight and general feel it has a high perceived value. When measured against melamine compounds it has similar properties but without the high cost. As a molding compound it can be compression or injection molded to produce a range of products. As a resin it is used for laminates, and binders for chipboard and plywood. As a foam it is used as insulation in wall cavities.

Close to the skin

Dimensions	445x387mm
Features	Good chemical resistance; Easy to color
	Warm; Good electrical insulation
	Scratch resistant; Stain resistant; High-gloss finish
	Cost-effective compared to melamine
More	www.perstorp.com, www.polypipe.com/bk
Applications	Electrical switch plates, junction boxes, toilet seats and covers, caps and closures for perfume bottles, buttons.

Burp

Everybody knows that reassuring slippery, soft plastic and that satisfying feeling as you seal down the lid ready for a picnic. That sound even has a name, the "Tupperware burp."

ICI first developed polyethylene in 1939, but it was a chemist at DuPont that first discovered how to injection mold it three years later. Soon after he set up Tupper Plastics. Although they were originally distributed in shops, it was not until Brownie Wise, the first door-to-door Tupperware lady, took them to the homes of American women that the products really took off.

Features	**Lightweight; Unbreakable**
	Relatively low cost
	Good resistance to hot and cold temperatures
	Excellent resistance to chemicals
	Well balanced relationship between stiffness, impact strength, and resistance to environmental cracking
	Crack resistant; Hygienic; Recyclable
More	**www.tupperware.com, www.basell.com**
	www.dsm.com, www.dow.com
Applications	**Chemical drums, carrier bags, car fuel tanks, blow-molded toys, cable insulation, furniture, wire insulation.**

Wondelier bowl set
Tupperware
Designer: Earl C. Tupper

Celebrity status

**Jumo Desk Lamp
Bakelite**

Bakelite was declared "the material of a 1,000 uses," when it was discovered in the first part of the twentieth century. It was one of the first plastics that gave designers freedom to create new aesthetics for products.

The name Bakelite is also the name of a company that produces phenolics and other materials. Phenolic resin does not work well with the addition of colors which is why phenolics are generally dark colors. Today phenolics are largely used as binders or adhesives in the production of board material and laminates. As a molding compound it can easily be reinforced by fillers and fibers that offer strength and prevent the product being too brittle. One of its modern-day uses is as handles for cookware.

Features	**Good heat resistance; Excellent flame resistance**
	High impact resistance; Low cost material
	Excellent dimensional stability; Nontoxic
	Good hardness and scratch resistance
	Outstanding electrical insulation
	Best suited to dark colors
	Brittle if molded in thin wall thickness
	Hard as a solid component
More	**www.bakelite.de, www.bakelite.ag**
Applications	**Brake linings, oasis foam support for flowers, binding for laminated wood panels, saucepan handles, door handles.**

Self-sealing

Supremecorq®

From Bordeaux to the Napa Valley and from Italy to Australia, wineries are turning away from natural cork in favor of plastic wine stoppers. The use of plastic corks was introduced to counter the occurrence of "corked" wine, when the wine has a mustiness and bad taste.

Made from a thermoplastic elastomer, used for its elastic sealing properties, the corks have a warm, slightly porous feel. This provides the sufficient leak and evaporation sealing qualities needed. The distinctive marbled effect results from the injection-molding process cooling at different rates. The corks have a self-sealing property, so when your corkscrew comes out of the cork the hole virtually seals up.

Dimensions	**Diameter 45 or 38mm**
Features	**Flexible; Good resistance to oil and chemicals**
	Good resistance to tearing and abrasion
	Easy to color; Recyclable; Can be painted
	Available in a range of Shore hardnesses
	Can be extruded, injection molded, and blow molded
	Keeps its properties at low temperatures
	Can be reinforced with glass fiber
More	**www.aestpe.com, www.supremecorq.com**
Applications	**Automotive, mechanical engineering, watch straps, sports shoes, shock absorbers, side trims for cars, hand tools, ski boots, offshore cabling, vacuum cleaner hoses, tires for shopping carts, grips for hand tools.**

231 Objects

232

Light work

Bic® products inhabit the world of everyday classics, where design and utility form seamlessly. Behind these icons of production and design lies the selection of materials that ensures that each of the four million Bic® lighters that are bought every day perform their intended task.

The biggest piece of material on the Bic® lighter is the acetal handle. With its use of bright color, it proclaims its use of plastic in an archetype of disposability. This is an engineering material used not for its aesthetics but for its functionality. It can be injection molded, extruded, blow molded, rotational molded, stamped, and machined. Comparable to polyester, PTFE, and nylons, acetals have some advantages over nylons at lower temperatures and are stiffer with better fatigue resistance. They also have a natural lubricant, especially in environments with a high moisture content.

Using DuPont's Delrin®, the Bic® lighter exploits this brand of acetal resin's high tensile strength, its durability, and its ability to withstand chemicals, including gasoline.

Dimensions	**60mm high**
Features	**Excellent impact strength and abrasion resistance**
	Excellent dimensional stability at a range of temperatures
	High stiffness
	Toughness at low temperatures
	Excellent resistance to chemicals
	Excellent dimensional stability
	Resilient; Low friction
	Good electrical-insulating characteristics
	Excellent fatigue resistance
More	**plastics.dupont.com**
	www.bicworld.com
	www.dupont.com/enggpolymers/europe/
	www.basf.com
Applications	**Can be used in diverse applications, from the base plate of a ski to the plastic buckles on rucksacks, where its high strength and moderate flexibility allow for its use as a clip. It is also used for plastic zips, golf tees, and gears. It can be used for mechanical components in food-packaging dispensers, washing machine handles, locking systems for removable frames in inline skates, gears in water sprinklers, and in replacing metals in window and door furniture, locks, handles, and latches. Its resistance to chemicals also makes it a good choice for perfume bottles.**

**Bic® Mini Tronic
disposable lighter
Steel and Delrin® plastic
Manufacturer: Bic**

Tough

There is one good reason why Lego® is made from ABS (acrylonitrile butadiene styrene). Apart from the fact that it has a high-gloss surface, and is cost-effective and easy to mold, it is also one of the toughest commodity plastics on the market. Have you ever known Lego® to break?

Lego® is one of the world's favorite toys. It is a product that has embraced plastic and has used advances in the material to evolve the brand into a series of products that keep up to date with children's imaginations and trends in toys.

On average, for every person on Earth there are 52 Lego® bricks. This proliferation has made it an icon of plastic. The bricks require an extremely high degree of manufacturing tolerances—0.002mm—for the "stud-and-tube" principle to work. That process keeps the 400,000,000 children and adults who play with Lego® bricks every year happy, and makes sure that they always, always stick together.

Features	High-impact strength, even at low temperatures
	Low cost
	Versatile production
	Good resistance to chemicals
	Good dimensional stability
	Scratch and flame resistant
	Can achieve a high gloss
	Excellent mechanical strength and stiffness
More	www.lego.com
	www.geplastics.com
	www.basf.com
Applications	Cellphone casings, shower trays, food processors, white goods, automotive consoles.

Lego® bricks
Designer: Lego
Manufacturer: Lego

234

Environmental PVC

Polyvinyl chloride (PVC) was one of the first widely available plastics, and it still occupies one of the largest areas of plastics consumed worldwide. However, PVC has developed a reputation as being an environmentally unfriendly material. These concerns come from several fronts. The first is the use of a chlorine compound that forms such a large part of PVC's composition. Unlike many other plastics, PVC is based on the use of approximately 50 percent petrochemicals; the other half is made of a chlorine-based compound. This marks one of its key advantages to producers, as the price of PVC is not as heavily based on price fluctuations of oil. However, the downside is that the production of PVC produces harmful dioxins.

The second main environmental issue is based on the use of the stabilizers and plasticizers in the production of the material. Stabilizers are used to impede degradation and plasticizers to increase flexibility. Both of these additives have problems. Stabilizers use heavy metals such as lead and barium, and plasticizers containing hormone disrupters.

There are moves to reduce these problems by the manufacturers: they can reduce the amount of dioxins being produced and can use organic stabilizers. The PVC industry's defense lies in what they claim is the low level of risk and likely exposure to these substances, and the fact that PVC has been used in the medical industry for many years for blood bags, where the use of plasticizers has been shown to extend the shelf life of blood.

Designed by Karim Rashid and using an environmentally friendly form of PVC, this dog toy is the alternative to a wooden stick. It expresses the idea that a product for a pet can also be something that the owner would enjoy possessing. This product has a fantastic shape that you would not mind having lying around at home.

Dog Bone
Designer: Karim Rashid
Manufacturer: For the Dogs

Dimensions	**200x200x35mm**
Features	**Easy to form; Cheap**
	Easy to color
	Water and chemical resistant
	Available in a variety of forms
More	**www.ecvm.org**
	www.karimrashid.com
	www.forthedogs.com
Applications	**Dip-molded bicycle handles, drain pipes, flooring, cabling, artificial skin in emergency burns treatment, sun visors, domestic appliances, raincoats, credit cards, inflatable toys. Unplasticized or rigid PVC (PVC-U) is used extensively in building applications, such as window frames.**

Clear and tough polyethylene terephthalate (PET) is one of the standard materials for drinks containers. Part of the polyester family, which also includes PBT and PETG, it is a crystal-clear plastic that is impervious to water and CO_2, which makes it ideal for this application. For bottles, it is often extruded with other materials to form sandwiches to increase its properties.

PET is common in drinks and food packaging: carbonated soft drinks have been sold in PET containers since the 1980s. However, due to beer being more oxygen- and carbon dioxide-sensitive, PET is not generally suitable for beer cans. Miller Brewing Company changed this with the launch of its first plastic beer bottle.

Features	Excellent resistance to chemicals
	Excellent dimensional stability
	Tough and durable; Good impact strength
	Excellent surface finish
	Color can be added for functional use, which provides excellent potential to extend the life of the product
More	www.ivv.fraunhofer.de
	www.socplas.org
Applications	Food, drinks, household cleaning products, and cosmetic packaging; display and decorative film; credit cards; clothing; auto body panels.

Bottling inspiration

Miller claims that the bottle keeps beer cooler longer than aluminum cans and as long as glass bottles. The bottle can be resealed and is unbreakable. There are five layers in each bottle: sandwiched in between three layers of PET are two layers of oxygen scavengers that stop oxygen getting in or out.

This active and intelligent packaging also uses color in a purely functional application. The technology was developed by the Fraunhofer Institute. Using nature as their inspiration, scientists have developed a plastic film and resin that acts as a UV light blocker. Using natural dyes from chlorophyll, the scientists have come up with a polymer with a hazy green translucency.

Reusable

Recycled PET has many uses, and there is a well-established market for this useful resin. By far the largest usage is in textiles. Carpet companies often use 100 percent recycled resin to manufacture polyester carpets in a variety of colors and textures. PET is also spun like cotton candy to make fiber filling for pillows, quilts, and jackets.

There is a certain fascination with drinks bottles made from PET, which means that people are always trying to find new uses for them. The bottles can be used to produce anything from bottle boats in Indonesia to water bottle rockets and bird baths. Empty bottles can be filled with cement and used as building bricks. In terms of the material, PETs represent one of the biggest areas of recycling, with the bottles being ground down to make carpets, fibers, and the filler for pillows and clothes: five two-liter PET bottles can yield enough fiber to make a ski jacket.

Features	**Recyclable (PET is one of the most recycled plastic resins)**
More	**www.eastman.com/Brands/Vitiva**
Applications	**Packaging, fillings for furnishings, sheets and ribbons.**

Is it a tape, is it a fabric, or is it a plastic molding? Whatever category it fits into, Hook and Loop (more commonly know as Velcro®) is a product that offers a great case study for a use of plastic.

The structure of Velcro® fibers is based on a mechanical fixing that is borrowed from nature, where the tiny hooks—commonly known as burrs—found on the end of some seed pods attach the seed more easily to an implantable surface that might brush past. It was this observation that led to Velcro®'s name being patented in the early 1950s by engineer George de Mestral: the name derives from the French words for velvet (velour), and hook (crochet).

Velcro® is used in both everyday contexts and advanced applications, allowing us to create new functions and products. It demonstrates the flexibility of plastics, and is unique in that it crosses the boundary between fabric, tape, and molded plastic. It also provides a case study because it appeals on so many levels: it combines the beauty of a simple observation into a product that has filtered into every possible area of application.

Variations on standard Velcro® include conductive Velcro® and a superstrong product branded under the name Dual Lock™. Instead of the hook-and-loop principle, this relies on a series of tiny mushrooms to join the two identical halves of the material together. In all versions of the material, this is a product that has brought new potential to the use of pliable plastics to be used as fixings.

Peelable fastener

Features	Strong; Lightweight
	Durable; Washable
	Available in a range of grades
More	www.velcro.com
	www.3m.com
Applications	Plastics have allowed for a mass of new types of fixing mechanisms that exploit the flexibility and resilience of plastics. Velcro® has an incalculable number of applications in which it is used, ranging from wearable to industrial. 3M, the makers of Dual Lock™, claim that its product has five times the tensile strength of standard Velcro®. It is used to invisibly attach doors and panels, headliners to cars, and in other applications that require superior strength.

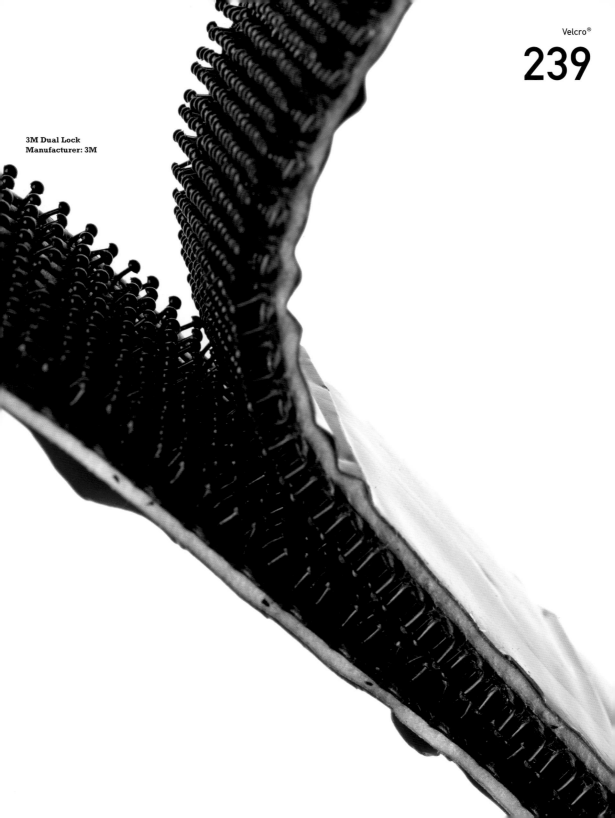

3M Dual Lock
Manufacturer: 3M

Presto Digital Bracelet
Designer: Scott Wilson
Manufacturer: Nike

Dimensions	**13x28.5mm diameter**
Features	**Extremely high bending strength**
	Excellent toughness
	Exceptional resistance to chemicals
	Lightweight
	High transparency
	Approved for water temperature up to 185°F (85°C)
More	**www.emsgrivory.com**
	www.studiomod.com
Applications	**Frames for safety glasses, lenses in optical glasses, instrument panels on cars, wing mirror housings, cellphone housings.**

Most products use plastic because it serves the purpose of the lowest common denominator. These are products that have no real relationship between material and aesthetics: they are merely the most convenient material in which to execute the form. But then there are products that celebrate the use of plastic, where the shape, color, material, and function combine to reveal an object that seems to have been born out of the material itself—a product that could not have been made with any other material. These Presto watches by Nike are beautiful products in which the use of plastic oozes the sensual quality of a high-gloss, polished, transparent surface.

Designer Scott Wilson is building up a collection of products that show a complete understanding of how plastic can be utilized in an intelligent and beautiful way within a range of everyday objects. Surprisingly, the candy-colored aesthetic is not cellulose as might be expected, but a custom-blended nylon 12, a material used in many sports eyewear frames.

The simple clasp contributes to the visual language of the form and exploits the toughness of nylon. To produce the watches, each band is molded, tumbled, and hand-polished to achieve the smooth finish and fluid "techno-organic" aesthetic.

High bending strength

Molded origami

Polypropylene (PP) has been a relatively new introduction to plastics. Originally developed in the 1950s, this commodity plastic occupies one of the largest segments in the plastic industry.

Polypropylene is as common in its molded form as it is in its die-cut sheet form, where it offers the designer a halfway point between folded paper and a fully tooled-up, molded product. Like a piece of clever origami, this fold-up coat hanger bridges these areas. As a raw material, polypropylene is relatively cheap and easy to process. It is also one of the best materials for creating live hinges, which is the prominent feature in this little gadget.

Dimensions	**Expands from 120x80 mm**
Features	**Can be flexed thousands of times without breaking**
	High heat resistance
	Excellent resistance to chemicals
	Low water absorption and permeability to water vapor
	Good balance between toughness, stiffness, and hardness
	Easy and versatile processing
	Relatively low cost
	Low density
	Low coefficient of friction
More	**www.basf.com**
Applications	**Garden furniture, food packaging, general household goods, dispensing lids for bathroom shower products, toothpaste tube lids, most products with an in-built hinge, bottle crates, tool handles.**

the surprising
FOLD HANGER

Thin and limp

PVC (polyvinyl chloride) is a material with many personalities, as it can be treated as thermoplastic, elastomer, and thermoset plastics. In its highly stiff and rigid form, it is known as the poor man's engineering plastic, but it can also be as flexible and limp as a piece of leather. Perhaps it was this analogy that prompted the use of PVC in this shoe by designer Yves Béhar.

The Learning Shoe, which was commissioned by the San Francisco Museum of Modern Art, explores the relationship between a wearable garment and a computer chip. Data is collected about the wearer's feet and walking style, and a smart sole adapts the shoe based on this information. Like a high-tech slipper from the next century, the form is like a seamless extension of the foot that wraps itself around the body like a piece of leather, while at the same time conforming to the soft, glossy language of plastic.

Dimensions	**285.75x114.3x63.5mm**
Features	**Easy to form and color**
	Cheap
	Water and chemical resistant
	Available in a variety of forms
More	**www.fuseproject.com**
Applications	**Dip-molded bicycle handles, drain pipes, flooring, cabling, artificial skin in emergency burns treatment, sun visors, inflatable toys. Unplasticized or rigid PVC (PVC-U) is used extensively in building applications such as window frames.**

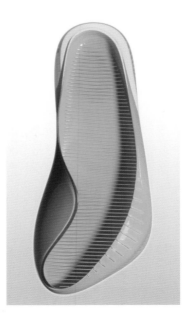

Learning Shoe
Designer: Yves Béhar
Client: San Francisco
Museum of Modern Art

247 Side Dishes

If ever a plastic was fun to play with this was one of them. Usually applied to T-shirts and spoons, you hold it for a couple of minutes over radiators and under taps and it changes color.

There are many types of color-changing technologies; thermochromic (changing color with temperature) and photochromic (changing color with ultraviolet light) are probably two of the most widely used. They can be applied as inks or as an impregnation into the material.

Thermochromic (TC) applications consist of two kinds of technologies: liquid crystal and leuco dyes. For applications where a high degree of accuracy is required, liquid crystal technology can give a greater control when regulating temperatures, which can usually be measured between -25°F to 250°F and can be sensitive enough to detect a change of 0.2°F. They start black and change to milky brown, red, yellow, green, blue, violet, and black if the temperature goes above its range. Leuco dyes offer less accuracy and are a cheaper alternative than liquid crystals. Photochromics (PCs) change color in response to ultraviolet light, and are most commonly found in sunglasses.

Features	**Can be printed; Offers high visual appeal**
	Adheres to a variety of substrates
	Can offer good safety potential
	Cost effective; Exciting appeal
	Advanced technology for a wide range of specifications
More	**www.colorchange.com/company.htm**
	www.interactivecolors.com
	www.solaractiveintl.com
Applications	**Thermometers, novelty products, baby products, mood rings, battery testers, toys, sunglasses, packaging for batteries.**

**Picnic containers
Solar Active™**

Color and heat

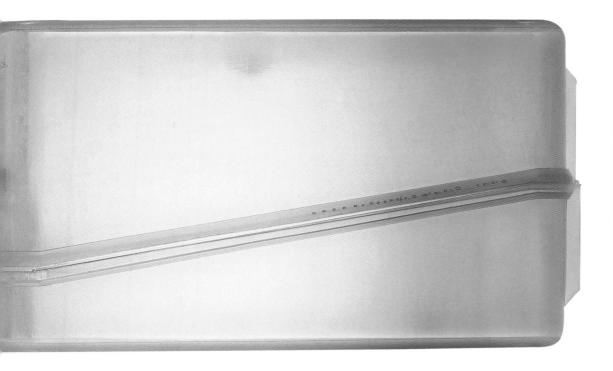

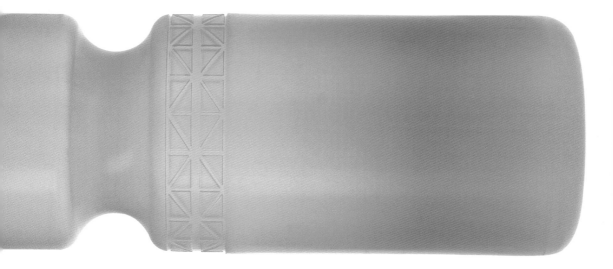

Features	Can offer high perceived value
	Available in a range of metallic colors
	Looks like metal but can be produced in forms that could not normally be made in metal
	Does not chip; Cost-effective
	Contained in the plastic rather than sprayed on
	Avoids costly additional painting
	Environmentally better as no paint necessary
More	www.geplastics.com/resins/visualfx/index.htm
Applications	Molded parts which can be made from a large number of polymers.

Faking it

Manufacturers are always looking for intelligent finishes that challenge our preconceptions. The paint finish Nextel was in vogue for a while, until we tired of it chipping off the corners of our hi-fis. Alas no more, plastics can now be made with effects built into the plastic so paint is no longer necessary.

DuPont have created a range of special-effect polymers that recreate the surfaces and finishes of other materials. One of these products is Ares which is supposed to "simulate the look of metal more realistically than previously possible." The effect is created by adding smaller-than-human-eye-sized metal flakes into the resins before processing. The resulting effect creates a greater sense of depth in the surface than paint would be able to achieve. It also doesn't chip.

Other effects in the DuPont stable include Light diffusion, a material that creates a translucent effect giving a sense of depth and mystery. Energy is a fluorescent resin available in a range of striking colors with different opacities. Marble speaks for itself and the subtle change of color in Intrigue gives a transient two-tone effect when the viewer moves in relation to the object.

253 New Combinations

**Plastic straw and
grapevine wire**

**Stretched nylon
stocking and resin**

This book is filled with examples of
products, furniture, advanced materials
and mass-produced, semiformed plastics
that you can source, buy, and use. The
objective is to inspire new uses for old
materials and provoke new applications
for emerging materials within a design
context. There is, however, another side
to plastics that lies somewhere between
the handmaking involved in craft objects
and the mass production in industrial
applications. This is a process of pure
experimentation, without any attachment
to a product—a place where new surfaces,
experiences, functions, and emotions can
be created by combining existing materials
both randomly and deliberately. This is an
experiment born purely out of the curiosity
to see what happens when, for example,
you combine wax with rubbers, iron fillings
with clear resins, or Latex with jelly.

**Fabric and
resin**

Without preconceptions and without
references to companies or finished
products, these inquiries into material
combinations have been put together with
a view to discovering new opportunities
for allying plastics with other materials.
These images are a feast of surfaces,
textures, colors, and other sensorial
elements, using a large palette of raw
ingredients. These experiments have been
put together to inspire and suggest new
functions, finishes, and tactile experiences
for you to digest and enjoy. Their only
purpose is to offer inspiration and new
recipes for both old and new materials.

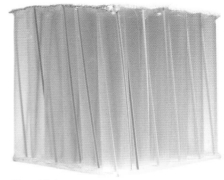

**Straw, fabric,
and card**

Acrylic sheet

Latex and silicone

**Latex, anti-bacterial fibers,
and acrylic**

Plastic mesh

Expanded foam

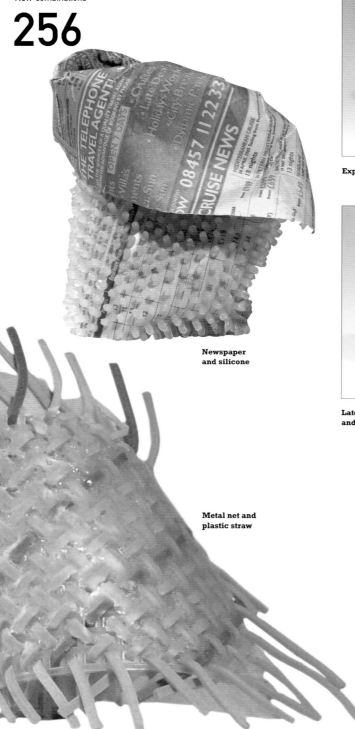

Newspaper
and silicone

Latex, acrylic color, wire mesh,
and polypropylene

Metal net and
plastic straw

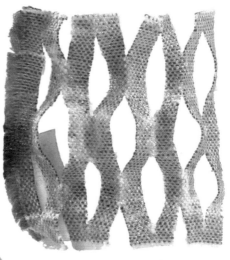

Fabric and resin

Knitted wool
yarn, latex,
and resin

Rice and tea leaves

Tin, rubber,
and latex

259 Appendices

260

Processing plastics

Any discussion about the use of plastics in products cannot ignore the manufacturing techniques that are used to process them. Many plastics can be produced by many of the processes. Choosing the right production process depends on many criteria: the shape of the product, the material requirements, the amount you can invest in tooling, and the number of parts you want to make. Injection molding requires high tooling investment but offers cheap unit costs, whereas rotational molding has lower tooling costs but high unit prices.

Here you will find some of the major processing techniques.

Blow molding	**A production process often featured on children's TV shows when they want to talk about mass production. Images are shown of tubes of plastic blown into a mold which are then sent running around a conveyor belt circuit. This process takes two forms: injection blow molding and extrusion blow molding.**
	Most plastic drink containers use the injection blow molding manufacturing process. The process is literally like blowing a balloon of plastic into a shape, which is determined by the inside shape of the mold. The use of injection molding allows for details such as threads to be formed, which will allow for the fitting of a lid.
	In injection blow molding, the process involves two stages. First, a tube is injection molded. This will normally include a thread for a lid, which is then rotated to the blow molding tool where hot air is injected into the tube. There it expands to fill the cavity of the final mold. Any textures and surfaces can be formed on the mold cavity and pressed onto the final part.
	Extrusion blow molding is a similar process, but instead of the part being injection molded at the beginning, it is extruded as a tube and pinched at both ends and then blown up to fill the mold.
Applications	**Milk bottles, carbonated drinks bottles, and containers.**

Calendering	The process of forming thin sheet material from plastic. It is the usual starting point for thermoforming sheets for shower curtains and plastic wrap. Calendering involves plastic pellets being fed through a series of heated rollers to form a sheet or film. Textures can be embossed into the sheet by texturing the rollers.
Applications	Acetate sheet, PVC sheet, shower curtains, and tablecloths.

Extrusion	The best way to understand extrusion is to think of plasticine toys for children, where you put the plasticine in a tub, turn the handle, and long, continuous lengths of the same shape are produced. This effectively is the same process as that used for modern mass-produced extrusions.
	The plastic pellets are poured into a hopper where they are heated and mixed with additives. A screw carries the melted plastic through the shaped die to produce continuous lengths of shapes with the same profile, which are then cooled by air or water.
	Extrusion is also used in metal parts, and as with plastic, sheets are cut to their desired length. Window frames, tubes, sheet, and film are all typical examples of the extruding process. Cost compared to injection molding is quite low. However, production is generally limited to minimum-order lengths.
Applications	Profiles, pipes, films, paper binders, window frames, Australian dollars, and curtain rails.

Compression molding	**Compression molding is used primarily for solid parts using thermosetting plastics. Compared with injection molding, extrusion, and other high turn-around production methods, compression molding is slower and more labor-intensive but has the advantage of lower tooling costs.**
	A measured amount of powdered resin is added to a two-part mold and the action of heat and pressure when the two molds are brought together cures the material. Good surface detail can be achieved with this process, but each piece will usually require some hand finishing.
Applications	**Melamine plates and toilet seats.**

Casting

Although with limited use in mass production, casting is one of the easiest and most accessible ways of producing simple solid plastic parts. Most hobby or craft shops will sell the basic molding and casting materials for this process to be completed at home.

Parts are initially made from any material, which can be cast to create a female mold. This mold will then be used to form the final part. Generally, casting materials are acrylic, epoxy, phenolic, polyester, and polyurethane resins. Molds can be created in rigid or soft materials. Resins are usually cured by the addition of a catalyst, and colors, additives, and fillers are added prior to casting.

Applications

Paper weights, sheets, and moldings.

Rotational molding

Rotational molding is used to create hollow, usually large-scale products. Its relatively low tooling costs make it an ideal process for low production-run pieces.

Precise quantities of powder or liquid are loaded into a two-part mold. The amount of material used determines the wall thickness of the final product. The mold is passed through a heating chamber and rotated along two axis. The plastic inside the mold melts, and the rotating motion allows for the plastic to cover the inside mold wall. The tool is cooled and the final product is released. The nature of this process means that the final part will have a uniform wall thickness. Because there is no pressure involved, this process is not ideally suited to parts that require fine detailing. The outside surface will replicate the wall of the mold, while the inside will have an inferior finish.

Applications

Storage drums, children's toy vehicles, and wheeled trash cans.

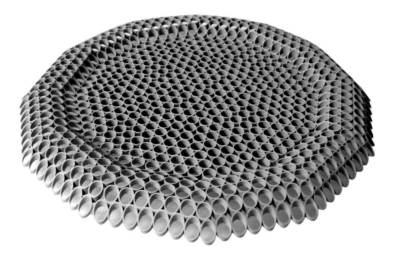

Injection molding

It allows designers virtually total freedom to create almost any imaginable form, and it is found in all areas of plastic product manufacture. Initially limited only to thermoplastics injection molding, it can now also be used for thermosets.

The process involves the polymer pellets being fed into the machine through a hopper, and then into a heated barrel. The heat from the barrel turns the plastic into a liquid resin, which is then injected into the mold. Co-injection molding involves the injection of two colors or materials into the same mold to create two distinct finishes or colors.

Injection molding is a high-volume, high tooling-cost process, where parts are produced at a rapid rate. Tolerances and details can be highly controlled. Unit costs are relatively low, but the process generally requires a much higher upfront tooling cost.

Applications

Computer housings, Lego, and plastic cutlery.

Gas-injection molding

In conventional injection molding thermoplastics are heated and injected into a mold. Channels in the mold act to cool the plastic part before releasing it from the mold. During cooling the part shrinks and moves away from the walls of the mold and, to compensate for this, more material is injected into the mold.

An alternative to this widely used method is to inject gas, usually nitrogen, into the mold cavity while the plastic is still in its molten state. This internal force counteracts the shrinkage by inflating the component to force and hold it in contact with the surface of the tool until it solidifies, resulting in parts with hollow sections or cavities.

Thermoforming

Thermoforming can be broken down into two main processes: vacuum forming and pressure forming. Both processes use pre-formed plastic sheet as the starting material. The principle of thermoforming relies on the use of either a vacuum or pressure to suck or push the plastic sheet over or into a mold.

In vacuum forming a mold is placed on a bed which can be lowered and raised. The plastic sheet is clamped above the mold and heated to the correct temperature, at which point the mold is raised into the soft material and a vacuum is applied. The sheet is then sucked over the mold.

The process of vacuum forming offers cost effectiveness over many other plastic-forming processes in the initial tooling investment. Because of the low pressure that is required, molds can be made from aluminum, wood, or even plaster. The accessibility of this process has meant that it is standard workshop equipment in most art and design workshops, where one-off experiments can be made.

Pressure forming requires a higher pressure than vacuum forming. Instead of a vacuum being used to pull the material over the mold, pressure is used to push it into either a male or female form. Pressure forming is better suited to products that require fine detail in the finishing.

Applications

Baths, boat hulls, and take-away lunch boxes.

Injection Blow Molding

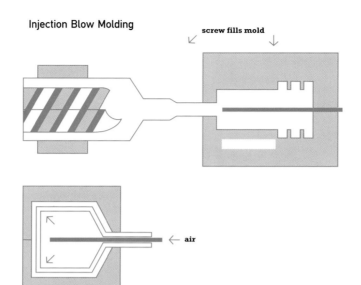

Extrusion Blow Molding

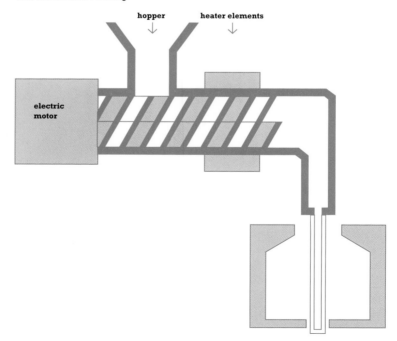

Monomer Casting/Contact Molding

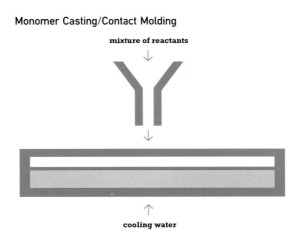

mixture of reactants

cooling water

Compression Molding

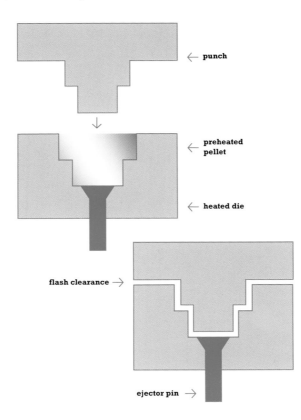

← punch

← preheated
pellet

← heated die

flash clearance →

ejector pin →

Extrusion

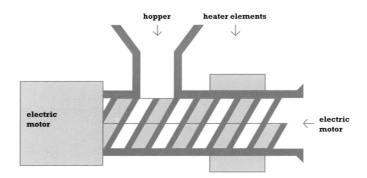

Injection Molding

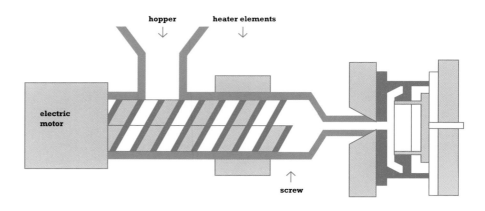

Extrusion of Blow Film

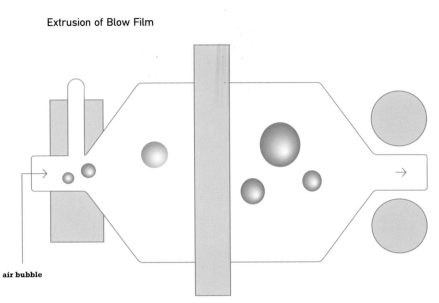

air bubble

Thermoforming

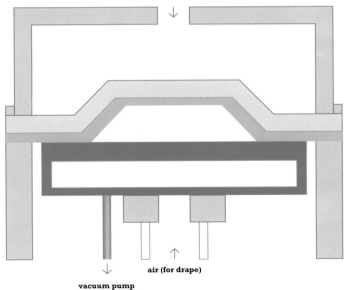

air (for pressure assisted)

vacuum pump

air (for drape)

Technical Information

Name	Trade Names	Applications	Properties
THERMOPLASTICS Acrylics **PMMA**	Perspex Diakon Oroglas Plexiglas	Signs, inspection windows, tail-light lenses, leaflet dispensers, lighting diffusers, hi-fi dust covers	Hard, rigid, glass-clear, glossy, weather-resistant, excellent for thermoforming, casting, and fabrication
Acrylonitrile Butadiene Styrene **ABS**	Lustran Magnum Novodur Teluran Ronfalin	Telephone handsets, rigid luggage, domestic appliance housings (food mixers), electroplated parts, radiator grilles, handles, computer housings	Rigid, opaque, glossy, tough, good low-temperature properties, good dimensional stability, easy to electroplate, low creep
Aramids	Kevlar®	Aerospace components, fiber reinforcement, high-temperature-resistance foams, chemical fibers, and arc welding torches	Rigid, opaque, high strength, exceptional thermal and electrical properties (up to 896°F/480°C), resistant to ionising radiation, high cost
Cellulosics **CA, CAB, CAP, CN**	Dexel Tenite	Spectacle frames, toothbrushes, tool handles, transparent wrapping, metallized parts (reflectors etc.), pen barrels	Rigid, transparent, tough (even at low temperatures), low electrostatic pick up, easily molded, and relatively low cost
Ethylene Vinyl Acetate **EVA**	Evatane	Teats, handle grips, flexible tubing, record turntable mats, beer tubing, vacuum cleaner hosing	Flexible (rubbery), transparent, good low-temperature flexibility (-94°F/-70°C), good chemical resistance, high friction coefficient
Fluoroplastics **PTFE, FEP**	Fluon Hostaflon Teflon	Nonstick coating, gaskets, packings, high- and low-temperature electrical and medical applications, laboratory equipment, pump parts, thread seal tape, bearings	Semi-rigid, translucent, exceptional low friction characteristics, superior chemical resistance, impervious to fungi or bacteria, high-temperature stability (500°F/260°C), low temperature (-256°F/-160°C), good weathering resistance, and electrical properties
Nylons (Polyamides) **PA**	Rilsan Trogamid T Zytel® Ultramid Akulon	Gear wheels, zips, pressure tubing, synthetic fibers, bearings (particularly for food processing machinery), nuts and bolts, kitchen utensils, electrical connectors, combs, barrier chains	Rigid, translucent, tough, hard-wearing, fatigue and creep resistant, resistant to fuels, oils, fats, and most solvents, can be sterilized by steam

Physical Properties			Producer	Resistance to Chemicals		Cost
Tensile modulas	2.9–3.3	N/mm²	ICI	Dilute Acid	****	$$
Notched impact strength	1.5–3.0	Kj/m²	ICI	Dilute Alkalis	****	
Linear coefficient of expansion	60–90	x 10⁶	Elf Atochem	Oils and Greases	****	
Max cont use temp	70–90	°C	Rohm	Aliphatic Hydrocarbons	**	
Specific gravity	1.19			Aromatic Hydrocarbons	*	
				Halogenated Hydrocarbons	*	
				Alcohols	****	
Tensile modulas	1.8–2.9	N/mm²	Bayer	Dilute Acid	****	$
Notched impact strength	12–30.	Kj/m²	Dow	Dilute Alkalis	****	
Linear coefficient of expansion	70–90	x 10⁶	Bayer	Oils and Greases	****	
Max cont use temp	80–95	°C	BASF	Aliphatic Hydrocarbons	**	
Specific gravity	1.04–1.07		DSM	Aromatic Hydrocarbons	*	
				Halogenated Hydrocarbons	*	
				Alcohols	*	
Tensile modulas	n/a	N/mm²	DuPont	Dilute Acid	n/a	$$$
Notched impact strength	n/a	Kj/m²		Dilute Alkalis	n/a	
Linear coefficient of expansion	n/a	x 10⁶		Oils and Greases	n/a	
Max cont use temp	n/a	°C		Aliphatic Hydrocarbons	n/a	
Specific gravity	n/a			Aromatic Hydrocarbons	n/a	
				Halogenated Hydrocarbons	n/a	
				Alcohols		
Tensile modulas	0.5–4.0	N/mm²	Courtaulds	Dilute Acid	**	$$
Notched impact strength	2.0–6.0	Kj/m²	Eastman Chemical	Dilute Alkalis	*	
Linear coefficient of expansion	80–180	x 10⁶		Oils and Greases	****	
Max cont use temp	45–70	°C		Aliphatic Hydrocarbons	****	
Specific gravity	1.15–1.35			Aromatic Hydrocarbons	*	
				Halogenated Hydrocarbons	*	
Tensile modulas	0.05–0.2	N/mm²	Elf Atochem	Dilute Acid	****	$
Notched impact strength	no break	Kj/m²		Dilute Alkalis	****	
Linear coefficient of expansion	160–200	x 10⁶		Oils and Greases	***	
Max cont use temp	55–65	°C		Aliphatic Hydrocarbons	****	
Specific gravity	0.926–0.950			Aromatic Hydrocarbons	*	
				Halogenated Hydrocarbons	*	
				Alcohols	****	
Tensile modulas	0.35–0.7	N/mm²	ICI	Dilute Acid	****	$$$
Notched impact strength	13–no break	Kj/m²	Ticoma	Dilute Alkalis	****	
Linear coefficient of expansion	120	x 10⁶	DuPont	Oils and Greases	****	
Max cont use temp	205–250	°C		Aliphatic Hydrocarbons	****	
Specific gravity				Aromatic Hydrocarbons	****	
				Halogenated Hydrocarbons	* variable	
				Alcohols	****	
Tensile modulas	2.0–3.4	N/mm²	Elf Atochem	Dilute Acid	*	$$
Notched impact strength	5.0–6.0	Kj/m²	Vestolit	Dilute Alkalis	***	
Linear coefficient of expansion	70–110	x 10⁶	DuPont	Oils and Greases	****	
Max cont use temp	80–120	°C	BASF	Aliphatic Hydrocarbons	****	
Specific gravity	1.13		DSM	Aromatic Hydrocarbons	****	
				Halogenated Hydrocarbons	*** variable	
				Alcohols	*	

KEY   * poor   ** moderate   *** good   **** very good

Name	Trade Names	Applications	Properties
Polyacetals POM	Delrin® Kematal	Business mechanical parts, small pressure vessels, aerosol valves, coil formers, clock and watch parts, nuclear engineering components, plumbing systems, shoe components	Rigid, translucent, tough, spring-like qualities, good stress relaxation resistance, good wear and electrical properties, resistant to creep and organic solvents
Polycarbonate PC	Calibre Lexan Makrolon Xantar	CDs, riot shields, vandal-proof glazing, baby feeding bottles, safety helmets, headlamp lenses, capacitators	Rigid, transparent, outstanding impact resistance (to -238°F/-150°C), good weathe resistance, dimensional stability, dielectric properties, resistant to flame
Polyesters (Thermoplastic) PETP, PBT, PET	Beetle Melinar Rynite Mylar Arnite	Carbonated drink bottles, business mechanical parts, synthetic fibers, video and audio tape, microwave utensils	Rigid, clear, extremely tough, good creep and fatigue resistance, wide-range temperature resistance (-40°F to -392°F/-40°C to 20(does not flow on heating
Polyethylene (High Density) HDPE	Hostalen Lacqtene Lupolen Rigidex Stamylan	Chemical drums, Jerry cans, toys, picnic ware, household and kitchenware, cable insulation, carrier bags, food wrapping material	Flexible, translucent/waxy, weatherproof, good low-temperature toughness (to -76°F/-60°C), easy to process using most methods, low cost, good chemical resistance
Polyethylene (Low Density) LDPE, LLDPE	BP Polyethylene Dowlex Eltex	Squeeze bottles, toys, carrier bags, high frequency insulation, chemical tank linings, heavy-duty sacks, general packaging, gas and water pipes	Semi-rigid, translucent, very tough, weatherproof, good chemical resistance, low water absorption, easily processed using most methods, low cost
Stamylan PP PP	Hostalen Moplen Novolen Stamylan PP	Sterilizable hospital ware, ropes, car battery cases, chair shells, integral-molded hinges, packaging films, electric kettles, car fenders and interior trim components	Semi-rigid, translucent, good chemical resistance, tough, good fatigue resistance, integral hinge
Polystyrene (General Purpose) PS	BP Polystyrene Lacqrene Polystyrol Styron P	Toys and novelties, rigid packaging, refrigerator trays and boxes, cosmetic packs and costume jewelry, lighting diffusers, CD cases	Brittle, rigid, transparent, low shrinkage, low cost, excellent x-ray resistance, free from odor and taste, easy to process
Polystyrene (High Impact) HIPS	BP Polystyrene Lacqrene Polystyrol Styron	Yogurt pots, refrigerator linings, vending cups, bathroom cabinets, toilet seats and tanks, closures, instrument control knobs	Hard, rigid, translucent, impact strength up to 7 x GPPS

Physical Properties			Producer	Resistance to Chemicals		Cost
Tensile modulas	3.4	N/mm²	DuPont	Dilute Acid	*	$$
Notched impact strength	5.5–12	Kj/m²	Ticona	Dilute Alkalis	****	
Linear coefficient of expansion	110	x 10⁶		Oils and Greases	*** variable	
Max cont use temp	90	°C		Aliphatic Hydrocarbons	****	
Specific gravity	1.41			Aromatic Hydrocarbons	*** variable	
				Halogenated Hydrocarbons	*****	
Tensile modulas	2.4	N/mm²	Dow	Dilute Acid	***	$$
Notched impact strength	60–80	Kj/m²	GE Plastics	Dilute Alkalis	***	
Linear coefficient of expansion	67	x 10⁶	Bayer	Oils and Greases	****	
Max cont use temp	125	°C	DSM	Aliphatic Hydrocarbons	**	
Specific gravity	1.2			Aromatic Hydrocarbons	*	
				Halogenated Hydrocarbons	*	
				Alcohols	N/A	
Tensile modulas	2.5	N/mm²	BIP	Dilute Acid	****	$$
Notched impact strength	1.5–3.5	Kj/m²	DuPont	Dilute Alkalis	**	
Linear coefficient of expansion	70	x 10⁶	DuPont	Oils and Greases	****	
Max cont use temp	70	°C	DuPont	Aliphatic Hydrocarbons	****	
Specific gravity	1.37		DSM	Aromatic Hydrocarbons	**	
				Halogenated Hydrocarbons	**	
				Alcohols	****	
Tensile modulas	0.20–0.40	N/mm²	Hoechst	Dilute Acid	****	$
Notched impact strength	no break	Kj/m²	Atochem	Dilute Alkalis	****	
Linear coefficient of expansion	100–220	x 10⁶	BASF	Oils and Greases	**variable	
Max cont use temp	65	°C	BP Chemicals	Aliphatic Hydrocarbons	*	
Specific gravity	0.944–0.965		HD DSM	Aromatic Hydrocarbons	*	
				Halogenated Hydrocarbons	*	
				Alcohols		
Tensile modulas	0.20–0.40	N/mm²	BP Chemicals	Dilute Acid	****	$
Notched impact strength	no break	Kj/m²	Dow	Dilute Alkalis	****	
Linear coefficient of expansion	100–220	x 10⁶	Solvay Chemical	Oils and Greases	**variable	
Max cont use temp	65	°C		Aliphatic Hydrocarbons	*	
Specific gravity	0.917–0.930			Aromatic Hydrocarbons	*	
				Halogenated Hydrocarbons	*	
				Alcohols	****	
Tensile modulas	0.95–1.30	N/mm²	Targor	Dilute Acid	****	$
Notched impact strength	3.0–30.0	Kj/m²	Montell	Dilute Alkalis	****	
Linear coefficient of expansion	100–150	x 10⁶	BASF	Oils and Greases	**variable	
Max cont use temp	80	°C	DSM	Aliphatic Hydrocarbons	*	
Specific gravity	0.905			Aromatic Hydrocarbons	*	
				Halogenated Hydrocarbons	*	
				Alcohols	****	
Tensile modulas	2.30–3.60	N/mm²	BP Chemicals	Dilute Acid	*** variable$	
Notched impact strength	2.0–2.5	Kj/m²	Atochem	Dilute Alkalis	****	
Linear coefficient of expansion	80	x 10⁶	BASF	Oils and Greases	*** variable	
Max cont use temp	70–85	°C	Dow	Aliphatic Hydrocarbons	****	
Specific gravity	1.05			Aromatic Hydrocarbons	*	
				Halogenated Hydrocarbons	*	
				Alcohols	** variable	
Tensile modulas	2.20–2.70	N/mm²	BP Chemicals	Dilute Acid	**	$
Notched impact strength	10.0–20.0	Kj/m²	Atochem	Dilute Alkalis	****	
Linear coefficient of expansion	80	x 10⁶	BASF	Oils and Greases	**	
Max cont use temp	60–80	°C	Dow	Aliphatic Hydrocarbons	****	
Specific gravity	1.03–1.06			Aromatic Hydrocarbons	*	
				Halogenated Hydrocarbons	*	
				Alcohols	* variable	

KEY   * poor   ** moderate   *** good   **** very good

Name	Trade Names	Applications	Properties
Polysulphone (Family) PES, PEEK	**Udel Ultrason Victrex PEEK**	**High- and low- temperature applications, microwave grills, electro/cryo surgical tools, aerospace batteries, nuclear reactor components**	**Outstanding oxidative stability at high temperature (328°F to 572°F/-200°C to 300°C), tran rigid, high cost, requires specialized processing**
Polyvinyl Chloride PVC	**Solvic Evipol Norvinyl Lacovyl**	**Window frames, drainpipes, roofing sheets, cable and wire insulation, floor tiles, hosepipes, stationery covers, fashion footware, plastic wrap, leather cloth**	**Rigid or flexible, clear, durable, weatherproof, flame-resistant, good impact strength, good electrical insulation properties, limited low-temperature performance**
Polyurethane (Thermoplastic) PU Thermosets		**Soles and heels for sports shoes, hammer heads, seals, gaskets, skateboard wheels, synthetic leather fabrics, silent running gear**	**Flexible, clear, elastic, wear-resistant, impermeable**
Thermoset plastics Epoxies EP	**Araldite Crystic Epicote**	**Adhesives, coatings, encapsulation, electrical components, cardiac pacemakers, aerospace applications**	**Rigid, clear, very tough, chemical resistant, good adhesion properties, low curing, low shrinkage**
Melamines/ Ure (Aminos) MF, UF	**Beetle Scarab**	**Decorative laminates, lighting fixtures, dinnerware, heavy-duty electrical equipment, laminating resins, surface coatings, bottle caps, toilet seats**	**Hard, opaque, tough, scratch-resistant, self-extinguishing, free from taint and odor, wide color range, resistance to detergents and dry cleaning solvents**
Phenolics PF	**Cellobond**	**Ashtrays, lamp holders, bottle caps, saucepan handles, domestic plugs and switches, welding tongs, and electrical iron parts**	**Hard, brittle, opaque, good electrical and heat resistance, resistant to deformation under load, low cost, resistant to most acids**
Polyester (unsaturated) SMC, DMC,GRP	**Beetle Crystic Synoject**	**Boat hulls, building panels, truck cabs, compressor housing, embedding, coating**	**Rigid, clear, chemical resistant, high strength, low creep, good electrical properties, low-temperature impact resistance, low cost**
Polyurethane (cast elastomers) EP		**Printing rollers, solid tyres, wheels, shoe heels, car fenders, (particularly suited to low-quantity production runs)**	**Elastic, abrasion and chemical resistant, impervious to gases, can be produced in a wide range of hardnesses**

Physical Properties			Producer	Resistance to Chemicals		Cost
Tensile modulas	2.10–2.40	N/mm^2	Amoco	Dilute Acid	****	$$$
Notched impact strength	40.0–no break	Kj/m^2	BASF	Dilute Alkalis	****	
Linear coefficient of expansion	45–83	x 10^6	Victrex	Oils and Greases	****	
Max cont use temp	160–250	°C		Aliphatic Hydrocarbons	** variable	
Specific gravity	1.24–1.37			Aromatic Hydrocarbons	*	
				Halogenated Hydrocarbons	*	
				Alcohols	****	
Tensile modulas	2.6	N/mm^2	Solvay Chemical	Dilute Acid	****	$
Notched impact strength	2.0–45	Kj/m^2	EVC	Dilute Alkalis	****	
Linear coefficient of expansion	80	x 10^6	Hydro Polymers	Oils and Greases	*** variable	
Max cont use temp	60	°C	Elf Atochem	Aliphatic Hydrocarbons	****	
Specific gravity	1.38			Aromatic Hydrocarbons	*	
				Halogenated Hydrocarbons	** variable	
				Alcohols	*** variable	
Tensile modulas	n/a	N/mm^2		Dilute Acid	n/a	$$
Notched impact strength	n/a	Kj/m^2		Dilute Alkalis	n/a	
Linear coefficient of expansion	n/a	x 10^6		Oils and Greases	n/a	
Max cont use temp	n/a	°C		Aliphatic Hydrocarbons	n/a	
Specific gravity		n/a		Aromatic Hydrocarbons	n/a	
				Halogenated Hydrocarbons	n/a	
				Alcohols	n/a	
Tensile modulas	n/a	N/mm^2	Ciba Geigy	Dilute Acid	n/a	$$$
Notched impact strength	n/a	Kj/m^2	Scott Bader	Dilute Alkalis	n/a	
Linear coefficient of expansion	n/a	x 10^6	Shell	Oils and Greases	n/a	
Max cont use temp	n/a	°C		Aliphatic Hydrocarbons	n/a	
Specific gravity		n/a		Aromatic Hydrocarbons	n/a	
				Halogenated Hydrocarbons	n/a	
				Alcohols	n/a	
Tensile modulas	n/a	N/mm^2	BIP Chemicals	Dilute Acid	n/a	$
Notched impact strength	n/a	Kj/m^2	BIP Chemicals	Dilute Alkalis	n/a	
Linear coefficient of expansion	n/a	x 10^6		Oils and Greases	n/a	
Max cont use temp	n/a	°C		Aliphatic Hydrocarbons	n/a	
Specific gravity		n/a		Aromatic Hydrocarbons	n/a	
				Halogenated Hydrocarbons	n/a	
				Alcohols	n/a	
Tensile modulas	n/a	N/mm^2	BP Chemicals	Dilute Acid	n/a	$$
Notched impact strength	n/a	Kj/m^2		Dilute Alkalis	n/a	
Linear coefficient of expansion	n/a	x 10^6		Oils and Greases	n/a	
Max cont use temp	n/a	°C		Aliphatic Hydrocarbons	n/a	
Specific gravity		n/a		Aromatic Hydrocarbons	n/a	
				Halogenated Hydrocarbons	n/a	
				Alcohols	n/a	
Tensile modulas	n/a	N/mm^2	BIP Chemicals	Dilute Acid	n/a	$
Notched impact strength	n/a	Kj/m^2	Scott Bader	Dilute Alkalis	n/a	
Linear coefficient of expansion	n/a	x 10^6	Cray Valley	Oils and Greases	n/a	
Max cont use temp	n/a	°C		Aliphatic Hydrocarbons	n/a	
Specific gravity		n/a		Aromatic Hydrocarbons	n/a	
				Halogenated Hydrocarbons	n/a	
				Alcohols	n/a	
Tensile modulas	n/a	N/mm^2	ICI	Dilute Acid	n/a	$$
Notched impact strength	n/a	Kj/m^2	Shell	Dilute Alkalis	n/a	
Linear coefficient of expansion	n/a	x 10^6	Dow	Oils and Greases	n/a	
Max cont use temp	n/a	°C		Aliphatic Hydrocarbons	n/a	
Specific gravity		n/a		Aromatic Hydrocarbons	n/a	
				Halogenated Hydrocarbons	n/a	
				Alcohols	n/a	

KEY   * poor   ** moderate   *** good   **** very good

Glossary

Additives	A wide range of substances that help in the processing of parts or in the physical and chemical properties of a final product. The additives are added to the basic resins by the resin supplier before being supplied to the production plant. Examples of additives include UV stabilizers, antibacterial additives, flame retarders, dyes and pigments, photochromics, reinforcing fibers, and plasticizers.
Blends	Blends can be used to tailor-make plastics with specific characteristics that cannot be achieved by a single polymer. They are a physical blend of two or more polymers to form materials with a combination of characteristics of both materials. Typical and common blends include: ABS/PC, ABS/polyamide, and PC/PP PVC/ABS. Blends are an additional form of tailoring polymers to those created by co-polymerization, and differ from co-polymers in that they are physical mixtures, not chemical.
Commodity plastics	Another way of dividing plastics is by categorizing them as either engineering plastics or commodity plastics. Commodity plastics have relatively low physical properties and are commonly used in the production of everyday low-cost products. This classification group includes vinyls, polyolefins and styrenes.

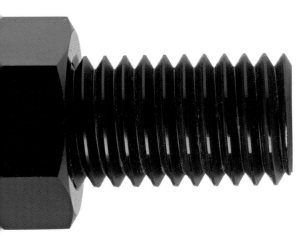

Co-polymers

The mixing of two or three compatible monomers, in order to form a new chemical compound which can be used to create a material that has a combination of the qualities of both monomers. This differs from a blend in that they are not physical but chemical mixtures.

Elasticity

The amount a material recovers to its original shape and size after it has been deformed. This is different to the testing of plastic behavior, which describes the way a material stretches and does not return to its original shape or size.

Elastomers

Elastomers are rubber-like materials but with far more processing potential. They can be processed in the same way as thermosetting materials. Elastomers may feel like rubbers but technically differ by their ability to return to their original length once they have been deformed, rubber being able to return to its original shape more quickly and easily.

Engineering plastics

There are a number of ways of classifying plastics: thermoplastic/thermoset, amorphous/crystalline. Paired with commodity plastics, engineering plastics are another way of categorizing plastics. They are generally a much higher cost with superior physical, chemical, and thermal characteristics and used in applications with demanding environments. They include acetals, acrylics, polyamides, and polycarbonates.

Fillers

Fibrous materials like glass and carbon which give enhanced mechanical properties like stiffness. Nonfibrous materials fillers such as hollow spheres, can be used to reduce the overall weight of a part.

Hardness

The ability of a material to withstand indentation and scratching. The most common tests are the Rockwell and Durometer tests, which are graded in Shore hardness from Shore A soft to Shore D hard. Examples of hard plastics include melamine, urea and phenolic formaldehydes, and PET. Low-density polyethylene and elastomers are examples of soft plastics.

Impact resistance

A material's ability to absorb energy. The final product is determined also by shape, thickness, and temperature. The Izod test for strength involves a sample of material being clamped to a base while a weighted pendulum is allowed to swing over a raised area of the sample, to see at what point the sample would snap.

Monomers

The individual molecules which, when joined together, form a polymer chain.

Plastic

The true definition of plastic does not describe a specific material but how a material acts. In common language, polymers are known as plastic due to the way they behave physically, i.e. their shape can be easily changed.

Polymer	A flexible, long chain of monomer molecules which display different characteristics according to the chemistry of the monomers and the size and shape of the molecules.	Thermoset plastics	One of the major ways of classifying plastics. Thermosetting plastics do not soften when heated and cannot be reused. Due to this characteristic they do not have the same processability of thermoplastics. As opposed to thermoplastics, their molecules form a cross-linked network that limits movement within the chains.

Polyolefins
This important group of polymers is made up of polyethylenes and polypropylene. Polyolefins are the largest produced plastics in the world, accounting for 45 percent of plastic production. Together with vinyls and styrenes, polyolefins are classified as commodity plastics.

Resins
Generally used to describe the basic polymerized material, e.g. polystyrene, ABS, which can also be described as polymers.

Tensile strength
The maximum pulling strain that can be applied to a material before it fractures.

Thermoplastic
Another major classification type for plastics. A material that by the action of heat can be softened, melted, and reformed without any change in properties. This means that off-cuts and scrap from manufacturing processes can be reground and reused, and products made from thermoplastics can be easily recycled. The shape of thermoplastic's molecules is linear, allowing them to move easily under heat and pressure.

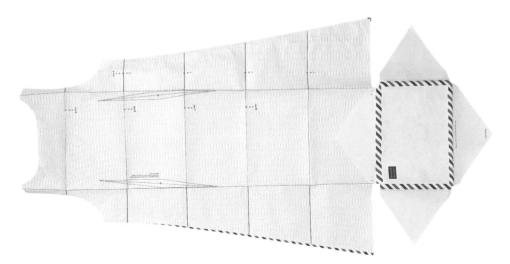

Abbreviations	ABS	**Acrylonitrile Butadiene Styrene**	PES	**Poly (Ether Sulphone)**
	ASA	**Acrylonitrilelstyrene Acrylate**	PET	**Polyethylene Terephthalate**
	ACS	**Acrylonitrile Styrene**	PI	**Polyimides**
	AES	**Acrylonitrile Styrene/EP (D) M Rubber**	PF	**Phenol-Formaldehyde (Phenolics)**
	BMC	**Bulk-Molded Compound**	PMMA	**Polymethyl Methacrylate (Acrylic)**
	CA	**Cellulose Acetate**	POM	**Polyoxymethylene (Polyacetal)**
	CAP	**Cellulose Acetate Propionate**	PP	**Polypropylene**
	DMC	**Dough-Molding Compound**	PPE	**Poly (Phenylene Ether)**
	EETPE	**Copolyester Ether Thermoplastic Elastomer**	PS	**Polystyrene**
	EP	**Epoxy**	PSU	**Polysulphone**
	EVA	**Ethylene Vinyl Acetate**	PTFE	**Polytetrafluoroethylene**
	HDPE	**High-Density Polyethylene**	PU	**Polyurethane**
	HIPS	**High-Impact Polystyrene**	PVC	**Poly (Vinyl Chloride)**
	LDPE	**Low-Density Polyethylene**	PVC/PVC	**Plasticized Poly (Vinyl Chloride)**
	MF	**Melamine Formaldehyde**	SAN	**Styrenelacrylonitrile**
	OTPE	**Olefinic Thermoplastic Elastomer**	SB	**Styrene Butadiene**
	PA	**Polyamide (Nylon)**	SBS	**Styrenelbutadiene-Styrene Block Co-polymer**
	PBT	**Poly (Butylene Terepthalate)**	SI	**Silicone**
	PC	**Polycarbonate**	TPU	**Thermoplastic Polyurethane**
	PE	**Polyethylene**	TPO	**Thermoplastic Polyolefin**
	PEEK	**Polyetheretherketone**	UP	**Unsaturated Polyester**

Index

Picture credits